THE RISE AFTER THE FALL

BY

SHALU

CONTENTS

The Many First Days

I am sitting in front of my laptop, staring at the blinking cursor as if it might type out the words I can't bring myself to say.

The room is still, yet the silence feels deafening, pressing against my chest like an unseen weight. My fingers hover over the keyboard, hesitant, lost between the past and the present.

Memories swirl around me, vivid and relentless, dragging me back to moments I wish I could forget—but they refuse to fade. My heart aches under their weight, and for a moment, I wonder if some stories are never meant to be written, only felt.

My parents have no idea what I'm doing right now. My mom, as always, must be thinking I'm wasting my time, probably scrolling through my phone or daydreaming about something useless.

But little does she know—I'm writing. I'm pouring my heart out, turning my past into words, reliving moments that once made me laugh, cry, and question everything.

This isn't just a story. It's a part of me.

It all started ten years ago, a time when life felt simpler, yet every moment carried a story of its own.

Life never lets me settle in one place for long. I kept moving from one city to another, switching schools, meeting new faces, and stepping into unfamiliar surroundings. Every place had its own stories, its own lessons.

Sometimes, I found myself blending in easily, while other times, I felt like a stranger in a world that wasn't mine.

With every move, I met different people—some who became friends, some who were just passing clouds in my journey. And in one of those chapters of my life, I met Soviet who was nothing less than weird in the best way possible.

Our bond wasn't like the usual friendships; it was built on an unexpected kind of fun—a silent, unspoken competition.

Every day in class, we would race to finish copying whatever was written on the board. It became our little challenge, a battle that only the two of us knew about.

No one else paid attention to this ridiculous contest, but to us, it meant everything. And no matter how hard I tried, she always managed to win. Every. Single. Time.

It's all part of school life—silly competitions, unexpected friendships, and moments that seem small but stay with us forever.

And there's one person I could never forget—Jamison, the son of our school's HM. Back then, he never missed a chance to complain about me, almost as if it were his favorite hobby.

Every little thing I did somehow ended up as a report to the teachers. I never understood why toppers found joy in doing such things—ufff! It used to frustrate me to no end. But life has a strange way of flipping things around.

From constantly being at odds, we slowly found common ground, and before I even realized it, the person who once seemed like my biggest enemy had become one of my best friends.

But life never stays the same, does it? Just when I thought I had figured things out, change knocked on my door again. A new city, a new school, and a new beginning awaited me.

I didn't know it then, but this next chapter would be different. And some friendships—no matter how strong—aren't always meant to last forever.

A FOREVER FRIEND

After years of hardship, we finally built our home in a quiet village nestled between towering mountains.

The mornings were filled with the gentle rustling of leaves, the sweet songs of birds, and the crisp, fresh breeze that carried the scent of blooming flowers.

The sky stretched endlessly, painted in hues of orange and pink at dawn, while the nights were adorned with countless stars, shining brighter than I had ever seen in the city.

It was a place where time seemed to slow down, where nature whispered its secrets, and where peace felt like a part of life itself.

And so, I had to change my school one last time. No more moving, no more new faces—this was where I would finally settle.

It felt strange, but at the same time, I was relieved that I wouldn't have to start over again.

There I met Rachel—my first best friend. With no siblings, she became my constant companion. We played, talked, and shared everything.

Rachel and I are still friends, even now, even after life pulled us in different directions after school. We were neighbors, always just a few steps away from each other, yet we rarely took pictures or even visited each other's homes.

It was never about capturing moments—it was about living them. Some friendships don't need proof to exist; they just do.

I had to move to a new school, one that was completely different from what I was used to.

The school was one of the most reputed in the town, known for its discipline and academic excellence. It had a structured system with strict rules that every student had to follow.

The dress code was mandatory, latecomers were not allowed without a valid reason, and punishments were common for even minor mistakes.

Unlike my previous schools, where things felt more relaxed, this place had a rigid atmosphere.

However, despite the strictness, the school was well-maintained, with spacious classrooms, a large playground, and dedicated teachers who ensured students stayed on track.

Rachel and I were placed in the same class, and from the very beginning, we became inseparable. Our friendship was filled with mischief—we would secretly pass notes during lectures.

Our constant chatter and playful antics soon caught the teachers' attention.

We were always up to something, laughing at the smallest things, and finding ways to make even the dullest classes entertaining.

Eventually, the teachers had enough of our distractions and decided to separate us in the next grade. From eighth standard onwards, Rachel and I were placed in different classes. Though we were disappointed at first, our friendship remains strong despite the distance.

One day, Rachel handed me a letter, her words etched not in ink but in her own blood—*"You are my first ever best friend, and I will never leave you for any reason."* In that moment, I realized the depth of her devotion, a promise sealed in a way that was both beautiful and terrifying.

Gosh, she must have been crazy to do that! I remember staring at the letter, my mind racing between shock and concern.

"Rachel, are you crazy? Who even does this?" I had asked, holding up the paper as if it might burn my fingers.

She just laughed, brushing it off like it was no big deal. But deep down, I knew—this wasn't just a dramatic gesture. It was her way of proving that, no matter where life took us, she meant every word she had written.

And in a world where friendships often faded with time, hers was the kind that refused to disappear.

SCHOOL DAYS TO REMEMBER

The school phase is one of the most important parts of a person's life. It's where we build our first friendships, experience our first failures and victories, and learn lessons that go beyond textbooks.

School gives us the joy of carefree days, the thrill of competitions, the nervousness of exams, and the excitement of lunch breaks filled with laughter. It teaches us discipline, responsibility, and teamwork, shaping us into who we become.

It's not just about education—it's about the memories, the bonds, and the moments that stay with us long after we leave those classrooms.

It's where we **make lifelong friendships, collect memories, and learn the hardest and sweetest lessons**. School gives us **laughter, fun, stress, excitement, and sometimes even heartbreak**.

It's a place where we **sneak snacks, whisper secrets, plan revenge on teachers who give too much homework, and share endless jokes**. But more than anything, it gives us a **treasure of moments that we will carry forever**.

One of the most thrilling experiences of school life is the **annual tour**. The excitement starts weeks before—**packing bags, making endless plans, and dreaming about all the fun**.

The **bus rides with friends, the loud singing, the dance battles, the unlimited junk food, and the carefree laughter**—those moments made the trip special. School trips are **not just about sightseeing but about creating stories** that we would later tell again and again with a smile.

It was the perfect way to **end our school journey**, leaving behind nothing but beautiful memories.

But school isn't just about fun and laughter. It's also the phase where we **face challenges and learn about the real world**.

It's the time when **most of us experience our first love, even if it's one-sided, secret, or just a beautiful feeling that never turns into words**. It's also the time when we **learn that not everyone around us is kind**.

And my school never missed a chance to throw me into the whirlwind of it all—friendships, challenges, laughter, tears, and lessons I never saw coming.

An Unexpected Sisterhood

After the teachers decided to put Rachel and me in separate classes, I sat there, feeling a little lost and sad. The familiar comfort of having her around was gone, and the classroom suddenly felt different—almost empty, even though it was full of students.

And then, just as I was sinking into my thoughts, the door creaked open. A girl walked in late, dressed not in the usual uniform like the rest of us, but in a colorful dress that made her stand out. She didn't say much, just quietly made her way to the last bench and took a seat.

That was the first time I saw Kanishka.

At that moment, I had no idea that this stranger would one day become such an important part of my life.

She was a hostel student, rarely visiting home, and at first, we were just classmates. But as time passed, we grew closer, sharing endless conversations and memories.

The first time I met her, I didn't think much of it. Just another face in the crowd, another student in a sea of unfamiliar names.

But life has a way of placing the right people beside you at the right time, and before I knew it, she wasn't just another name—she was my person.

Our friendship wasn't built in a day. It wasn't loud or dramatic; it was a quiet, steady presence that grew stronger with time.

We found joy in the simplest things—stealing moments of laughter between classes, sharing snacks like they were precious treasures, whispering about dreams too big for our small world.

We weren't just friends; we were a team. We covered for each other when one of us was late, wrote each other's notes when one of us zoned out, and fought over the dumbest things just to end up laughing about it the next minute. If school was a battlefield, we were each other's shield.

There was something about her presence that felt unshakable, like the sky above—constant, endless, and full of stars. Maybe that's why I never thought I could lose her. Maybe that's why I didn't see the storm coming.

For seven years, our friendship felt unbreakable—until it wasn't.

Let's stay here, in this moment, where the laughter still echoes, and the stars are still shining.

THE STOLEN YEARS

School was always a second home—a place filled with laughter, fights, last-minute homework, and endless fun.

But for us, the "Corona Batch," everything changed overnight. One day, we were sitting in our classrooms, passing chits, pretending to listen to lessons, and making secret weekend plans.

Next, we were locked inside our homes, staring at screens, trying to convince ourselves that online classes could ever replace the real thing.

At first, it felt like a blessing—no school, no early alarms, no rushing to get ready. Waking up late, watching movies, spending hours on our phones—it was fun. "Just two weeks of lockdown," they said. It felt like an unexpected vacation.

But as days turned into weeks, and weeks stretched into months, the excitement faded into something else—something empty. The same four walls, the same routine, the same loneliness.

The urge to step outside, to feel the breeze, to laugh with friends—all of it became distant, like a memory from another life.

The world outside was crumbling. Every day, news channels showed a reality more terrifying than any nightmare. People struggling to breathe, families losing loved ones, hospitals running out of beds. The roads were empty, yet the weight of suffering filled the air.

For us, students, life was frozen. Classes became just a screen, voices without faces, messages instead of whispers.

Even birthdays were celebrated through lagging video calls, where smiles felt forced, and silence stretched longer than words.

We thought staying home would be easy. But no one warned us about the loneliness, the fear, the helplessness of watching the world suffer from behind locked doors.

The days blurred into each other, and time lost its meaning. And somewhere in those stolen years, we grew up without realizing it.

To the families who lost their loved ones during those dark times—no words can truly fill the space they left behind. The world may have moved on, but your pain is still real, your grief still valid.

Your loved ones were not just numbers in a statistic; they were someone's parent, sibling, child, or friend. They had dreams, laughter, and memories that will never fade.

Though they may not be here physically, they live on in the love they shared, in the stories you tell, and in the hearts they touched.

Healing takes time, and some wounds never fully close—
but you are not alone. Your pain is seen, your loss is
remembered, and your strength is admired.

May you find peace in their memories and comfort in knowing
that love never truly leaves—it just changes form.

BACK, BUT NOT THE SAME

After months of being trapped within four walls, staring at screens, and pretending to "study" while actually scrolling through random stuff, we finally got the news—we were going back to school.

But it wasn't the same school life we had left behind.

The excitement of meeting my friends again was real, but so was the awkwardness. We had spent almost a year indoors, and suddenly, stepping into a classroom felt like stepping into an unfamiliar world.

Some of my friends had become so lean, while others had gained weight—LOL, almost unrecognizable!

Yeah, things were definitely not the same as before. When we finally stepped back into school, it didn't feel like the place we had left behind. Masks covered our faces, hiding smiles that were once shared freely.

The desks were spaced apart, and strict distance was maintained, making even the simplest conversations feel distant.

Lunchtime, which used to be filled with laughter and shared snacks, felt empty. We weren't allowed to exchange food, no more "one bite for me, one bite for you."

It was strange, almost like we were in the same place but living in a completely different world.

But there was something different. Some seats remained empty, a reminder of those who never got the chance to return. Life had moved forward, but the scars of loss remained in many hearts.

Then came the best (or worst) part—**the board exams**. With all the chaos, it felt like the universe had given us a free pass.

The pressure was there, but let's be real—compared to what the previous batches had gone through, we definitely got the easier route.

Some called us the "Corona Batch," as if we were a special edition of students who had somehow dodged the academic struggles.

And yet, in that short time, we made memories—laughing during revision hours, helping each other (sometimes with answers too), and feeling the thrill of writing the final exam papers. It wasn't the grand farewell we had imagined for our 10th grade, but it was an experience we'd never forget.

THE UNSCRIPTED CHAPTER

Soon, things started to return to normal after the long, isolating months of the pandemic. Schools reopened, and we were finally back in the classrooms we had missed for so long.

But something had changed—life wasn't exactly as it was before. The carefree school days had been replaced with a new seriousness. Masks came off, but the weight of expectations settled in.

Higher secondary felt like a fresh start yet a tough transition. The shift from **secondary school to higher secondary** wasn't just about new subjects; it was about balancing fun with newfound responsibilities, where laughter filled the hallways, but so did the pressure of what lay ahead.

The pressure of choosing the right stream, dealing with tougher subjects, and the thought of board exams lurking in the distance made everything feel different.

This was the year I met **one of the best teachers of my life—Sarguneshwaran sir, my chemistry teacher**. Before meeting him, I **never thought chemistry could be interesting**, but he changed my perspective completely.

He wasn't just a teacher; he was more like **a brother**, someone who made learning fun and enjoyable.

Apart from studies, he even attempted to set a record with one of our students by making them recite all the elements of the periodic table in one go!

But beyond my department, there was **our Computer Science Sir**—though he didn't directly teach me, our bond was special.

Some teachers make a lasting impression not because of the subjects they teach but because of the way they connect with students.

Talking to him felt easy, like speaking to someone who genuinely understood and cared.

He had this way of explaining things that made even random conversations feel meaningful.

One thing I would never forget in my high school was my Zoology period.

If it was a **Zoology period**, there was one golden rule I followed—**disappear**. Since I sat on the **last bench**, it was the perfect hiding spot.

The moment our Zoology ma'am started her lecture, I would slowly slide down my bench, rest my head on my bag, and **enter nap mode**. It was my personal escape from the endless talk of biological classifications and animal kingdoms.

And trust me, I **never broke this rule**. No matter what, I would **strictly** follow my routine—head down, eyes shut, and let the lecture turn into background noise.

The best part? **I never got caught.** Maybe because I had mastered the art of waking up just in time or because she had given up on me altogether. Either way, those periods were my **official recharge time**.

But let's be honest—who wouldn't fall asleep when the entire class felt like a lullaby of scientific names?

I also had a favorite spot in my school—the third pillar in front of the class. It had the best view of the entire school, and during my last two years of school life, it became my go-to place.

I spent countless hours there, sharing stories, secrets, and laughs with my friends. That pillar may not have been there for my entire school life, but it surely witnessed the best part of it.

At first, Kanishka was just another classmate, but soon, she became one of my closest friends. Along with Akshitha, we became an unbreakable trio throughout my higher school years.

Amidst all the chaos and fun of my higher school years, there was one person who always stood in the middle whenever storms arose between me and Kanishka—Akshi.

She was the one who tried to **hold things together** when I had fights with Kanishka. No matter how heated our arguments got, she would step in, trying to **calm us down, reason with both sides, and bring back the peace.**

She wasn't the type to take sides—**her loyalty was to our friendship itself**. While Kanishka and I threw words at each other, Akshitha would be there, **patiently listening, trying to make us see sense**.

Sometimes, I wondered **how she even had the patience** to deal with our drama, but she never gave up on either of us.

Beyond being a peacemaker, she was **a kind and dependable friend**. She would always **check up on me** after a fight, making sure I wasn't overthinking things.

If I ever needed someone to talk to, she was always there, **offering words of comfort or just sitting in silence**— whichever I needed at the moment.

Friendships can be messy, but **having someone like Akshi made it a little easier to handle**.

The three of us **shared everything—our joys, our secrets, and even our fights**.

It wasn't too serious, and it wasn't too reckless—it was just right. And I wouldn't trade those moments for anything.

A Year to Remember

Here, the final phase of my school life—my higher secondary years—was the most memorable and emotional. The special class periods had a charm of their own.

The entire school would be silent, but we, the higher-grade students, would be there, filling the corridors with our whispers, laughter, and stolen snack breaks.

It was also the time I met two teachers who left a lasting impact on me—Salma Kabir ma'am (my English teacher) and Anandi ma'am(my math teacher).

They always believed in me, supported me, and treated me like a gem. Somehow, I felt like I was their favorite student. Their encouragement made me feel capable and strong.

Singing was the best thing I did all the time. Whether it was during breaks, free periods, or even in the middle of a boring lecture, music was our escape.

My favorite moment was when I confidently rapped a song, and out of nowhere, two of my friends jumped in, syncing perfectly with me.

The energy in the room shifted, our voices grew louder, and soon the whole class turned to watch us. Some laughed, some cheered, and a few even clapped along.

We didn't stop there—our singing wasn't just for fun among ourselves. We even sang with our physics sir, who secretly enjoyed the madness. And then there was Salma ma'am, who, despite being a good singer, would never admit it.

Of course, we didn't let that stop us—we practically dragged her into singing during Teacher's Day, turning the whole event into a memory we'd cherish forever.

My school rarely conducted celebrations, and whenever there was one, it felt like a once-in-a-lifetime event. Annual days, cultural fests, or even small functions were a rarity, making them all the more special.

And the best part? Bunking classes during dance practice, even though we weren't part of the performance! Whenever there was an event, the dance team would get special practice sessions, and that was the golden opportunity for the rest of us.

Sneaking out of class, pretending we had something important to do, and then sitting in the auditorium or the practice hall, just watching and enjoying—it was a different kind of thrill.

Sometimes, we'd even join the dancers for fun, laughing at our own awkward moves before running back when a teacher showed up. Those stolen moments, the shared glances with friends, and the excitement of getting away with it made those rare celebrations even more unforgettable.

But the final phase of my school life wasn't just about studies and teachers—it also gave me one of my proudest moments.

One morning, during a special class in the third-floor hall, all the higher secondary students were gathered for a maths period. Suddenly, a girl fainted. Everyone stood around her, panicking, trying to wake her up, but no one took the step to actually carry her downstairs.

At that moment, I don't know why, but a **voice inside me said, "Go help her."**

Without thinking twice, I **ran towards her, lifted her up in my arms, and carried her all the way to the ground floor**. The entire school was **shocked**. People were **whispering about it**, and from that day, I became **a little popular in school for this heroic action**.

Despite all these moments, **school wasn't always filled with happiness**.

Then, the final exams were around the corner, and as expected, the pressure was building up. But did that stop us from having fun? Not at all.

Every single time, we would casually ask for a separate classroom to study, and somehow, they actually gave us one! But if only they knew the truth—studying was the last thing on our minds.

That little room became our playground, our hideout, our world.

Between the pages of textbooks, we hid laughter; between the lessons, we wove stories.

We would imitate our teachers with exaggerated voices, acting like we ruled the school, mimicking their mannerisms so perfectly that even we couldn't hold back our laughter.

And when boredom struck, we turned the classroom into a concert stage, singing at the top of our lungs, dancing like nobody was watching, like the walls themselves were our audience.

Those four walls held our wildest, most carefree moments— memories that even time wouldn't dare erase.

Teacher's Pet and the Unfair Favors

There are always a few students in every class who seem to have an invisible shield protecting them from punishments, scoldings, or bad grades.

These students—often called the teacher's pets or puppets—hold a special place in the teacher's eyes, whether because of their constant obedience, eagerness to help, or just their knack for always being in the teacher's good books.

They are the ones who never forget to wish the teacher "Good morning" in the sweetest voice, the first to raise their hands when volunteers are needed, and the ones who willingly carry the teacher's books or fetch their lunch from the staffroom.

They act as informers, always quick to remind the teacher about pending assignments, much to the frustration of the rest of the class.

But it doesn't stop there. The real advantage of being a teacher's puppet lies in the privileges they receive. If they forget to submit their homework, the teacher brushes it off as a rare mistake.

If they talk in class, they get a friendly warning instead of being made to stand outside. Their answers in exams, even when mediocre, seem to earn them higher marks.

While other students get scolded for being late, these favored ones receive nothing more than a gentle reminder.

When there's a need to assign responsibilities like class monitor, event coordinator, or any prestigious role, their names are the first to be considered. Their opinions hold weight, and their mistakes are easily forgiven.

The rest of the class can only watch in frustration, knowing that no matter how much effort they put in, they may never receive the same special treatment.

And then there's the most amusing part—when these students act as the teacher's spies. They report any mischief happening behind the teacher's back, sometimes exaggerating details, knowing that their loyalty will only strengthen their favored position.

While some students genuinely earn this favor through hard work and discipline, others simply master the art of staying in the teacher's good books.

Whether it's fair or not, this kind of favoritism exists in almost every classroom, shaping the way students perceive authority and justice from a young age.

When School Felt Like Hell

School life is not only about fun, laughter, and exams—it's also where we face hard times that shape us. It's the time when we learn that not everyone is as good as they pretend to be and that sometimes, the biggest lessons come from outside the textbooks.

Sometimes, younger people behave **more maturely**, while **older people fail to**. My **school hostel warden** was one such person. She **never missed a chance to spoil my name**. Somehow, she entered my life just to **show me that not all people are sweet**.

She made me cry, yet the next day, she would **talk to me like she had never said anything bad behind my back**. The things she did and the words she spoke **were too painful for my 16-year-old self to understand**.

That's when I realized—**some people exist only to teach us who we should never become.**

And finally, it was the last board exam—the last moment of being a school student. I couldn't believe that after this, I would no longer see my friends, my teachers, or even my favorite pillar where I had spent countless hours.

Everywhere I turned, posts and reels about the end of school life flooded my feed. They all said the same thing—*"You*

*will drop your pen for the last time, and that's where your
school life ends."*

I didn't want to believe it. But the night before the final
exam, reality hit me like a storm. Tomorrow, everything will
change.

I found myself crying, and once I started, I just couldn't stop.
It wasn't just sadness—it was the weight of every memory,
every laughter, every moment slipping away.

Then came the last exam. Sitting in that hall, my hands felt
weak, my heart pounded, and my vision blurred with unshed
tears. Somehow, I finished my paper, but as soon as I
stepped out and saw my friends' faces, it all became real.

I ran to them, hugged them, and broke down.

And just like that... I wasn't a school student anymore.

Later, we returned to pack up our things, but that moment—
standing there for the last time—was beyond words. It
wasn't just an ending; it was the closing of a chapter we
could never rewrite.

No matter how much we tell ourselves we're ready, nothing
prepares us for the moment we say goodbye to school life.

And just like that, the final bell rang—not just for the day, but for an entire chapter of our lives. The corridors that once echoed with our laughter would now carry only the whispers of memories, the desks where we carved our names would sit untouched, waiting for new hands to leave their mark. We had spent years here, growing, dreaming, falling, and rising again, but no one had warned us that leaving would feel like losing a part of ourselves. Maybe one day, we'd return, searching for the past in empty hallways, hoping to hear our younger selves in the distant echoes. But deep down, we knew—time had already closed its doors, leaving us standing on the other side, holding nothing but memories that would never fade, yet could never be relieved.

THE SCORE THAT SPOKE

After a long wait, results day finally arrived. I had only put in 50% of my effort, yet I still managed to secure a decent score—518 out of 600. A small smirk appeared on my lips, not out of surprise, but because I had almost predicted it.

And for those who doubted me? Well, this was proof that I was never to be underestimated.

I always had a way of grasping things quickly. If I had truly given it my all, I wouldn't have just done well—I would have set a new standard. But honestly, why stress when I could still get the job done in my own way?

I was a proud backbencher. We weren't the ones chasing ranks, but we always had our own way of standing out.

Masters of last-minute studying, experts at turning dull lectures into fun moments, and the ones who knew how to make the most out of school life—we weren't just students, we were storytellers of our own journey.

A Bond That Grew

Back in school, Sanjay and I were from different batches, so our paths rarely crossed. We were just two people who occasionally saw each other in the halls or during school events, but we didn't really know each other.

There were no regular greetings or deep conversations—just brief moments where we would smile or nod in passing.

It wasn't until after I finished my high school that we started talking more. Somehow, we reconnected, and from there, our conversations became more frequent.

There was this strange pull to share thoughts and experiences that had been bottled up during those school years. As we spent more time talking, I began to realize how much we had in common.

What struck me the most was how easily we became close. We shared stories of what life had been like after school—how everything had changed, what we'd learned, the challenges we faced.

Slowly, those casual chats turned into something much deeper.

The trust began to grow, and Sanjay became someone I could turn to, someone I could confide in without hesitation.

What made him even more special was that whenever I felt low or lost, Sanjay was the one who was always there for me.

No matter what, he would listen without judgment, offering comfort and support, helping me get through those tough times. It wasn't just about the happy moments; it was about knowing he would stand by me through the hard ones too.

Somehow, in the midst of everything, Sanjay became my best friend—the person who I could always count on.

It was odd, at first, to go from not really knowing someone in school to sharing my thoughts with them so openly. But somehow, it felt natural. Sanjay was always a great listener, never rushing to speak, just letting me share whatever was on my mind.

It was this quiet understanding that built our friendship, and before long, he was the person I trusted the most.

Looking back, it's funny how life works. We went from strangers to the closest of friends, and I couldn't have predicted how much he would come to mean to me. What started as a few random encounters turned into a bond that has lasted through the years.

And I believe, in the end, everyone will find a person like Sanjay in their lives. Someone who listens without judgment, someone who shows up when you least expect it but need them the most.

That rare connection, where trust and understanding flow effortlessly, is something we all deserve. And I'm lucky enough to have found mine.

DAYS OF NOTHINGNESS

I had a long break after completing school. No exams, no early mornings, no last-minute cramming—it was pure freedom. I could sleep in, binge-watch movies, and scroll endlessly on my phone without a single worry.

But as the days passed, the excitement wore off. The routine I once complained about suddenly felt like something I missed. No school meant no daily chaos, no classroom fun, no silly fights, and no shared lunch breaks. The days felt slower, and boredom crept in.

Some of my friends moved to different cities, others got busy planning their college lives. It was a strange phase— stuck between childhood and adulthood, waiting for the next big chapter to begin.

And then, the dreaded career talk began.

Relatives, neighbors, even people who barely knew me suddenly had the same set of questions: "What course are you taking?" "Which college?" "What's your future plan?" As if life came with a pre-written script we were supposed to follow.

The truth? I had no idea.

As kids, career dreams were simple—watch a movie, get inspired, and boom, that's the new dream.

One week, I wanted to be a doctor. The next, a detective. Then came the astronaut phase, followed by the dream of being a business tycoon.

But these dreams never lasted long. Back then, it didn't matter. We could dream without the weight of reality.

Now? Choosing a career wasn't just a fantasy anymore—it was real. Unlike childhood, where we could switch dreams overnight, this time, it felt like a permanent decision. And that was terrifying.

There was always that one friend who had everything figured out, making the rest of us feel even more lost. Some were excited about their chosen paths, some were just going with the flow, and then there were people like me—stuck between passion and practicality.

Late-night thoughts turned into overthinking sessions. One moment, I felt confident about my decision. Next, I was second-guessing everything. "Am I making the right choice?" "What if I regret this later?" It was an endless cycle.

Meanwhile, all I wanted was to breathe, take my time, and maybe squeeze in a nap in between.

But after jumping from one dream to another, I finally found something that felt right. It wasn't a sudden realization, but a slow acceptance that this was where I truly belonged. The pressure didn't vanish overnight, but at least I wasn't lost anymore.

I never took the computer science group in school, yet here I am, deep into coding, cybersecurity, and AI—things I never officially studied but always felt drawn to.

Back then, I didn't even have my own phone, so I'd sneak in a few minutes on my mom's whenever I got the chance. I'd try to learn, but to her, it was just another distraction. "Stop wasting time on this and study something useful!" she'd say.

Little did she know, the very thing she thought was a waste of time would become my passion, my career, my future.

While everyone seemed to have their paths figured out, I stood at a crossroads—unsure, but hopeful. People gave advice—some practical, some completely unrelated to my interests. But deep down, I knew I had to choose what felt right, not what was expected.

So, I took a path that wasn't planned, wasn't traditional, but felt like home.

Looking back now, I realize—sometimes, the things that seem small and insignificant turn out to be the most defining moments of our journey.

A Choice, Not Mine

I had everything planned. I wanted to join college with my best friend. We had dreamt of sitting together in lectures, roaming around the campus, bunking classes, eating from the same plate in the canteen, and vibing together.

But fate had other plans. My parents had just one condition—I should **not** stay in a hostel. No matter what, they wanted me to come home every day.

I started searching for colleges nearby, hoping to find something decent. But finding a good college within my home-travel boundary was like searching for a drop of water in a desert.

Every option I had was either too far or didn't match my expectations. I was still confused about where to go when suddenly, one day, my dad took me to a college I had never even considered.

The journey itself was exhausting—it took **one and a half hours** to reach from home. And when I arrived, my heart sank.

The moment I stepped in, I knew—this wasn't the kind of college you dream about.

The buildings looked old, untouched by time, with walls that seemed to have absorbed years of silence and boredom. The classrooms were dull and lifeless, with wooden benches that had scratches and carvings of past students' frustrations.

The air itself felt heavy, as if even the college itself knew how boring it was.

And then came the biggest disappointment—**no culturals, no fests, no fun.** The place had no excitement, no lively energy, nothing that screamed "college life." Just strict rules, a suffocating orthodox environment, and lifeless schedules.

Students walked around with blank faces, their eyes carrying the weight of routine and restrictions. Creativity? Buried. Freedom? A myth.

And as if all that wasn't enough, we had to wear a **boring uniform.**

A **uniform. In college.**

I mean, school is over! College was supposed to be the place where we finally got to wear what we liked, express ourselves, and feel a little grown-up.

But no, here I was, stuck in an outdated uniform that just added to the misery. It felt like I was back in school, except this time, without any of the fun.

The worst part? I had no choice.

I had to accept this college, even though it was the last place I wanted to be. **This was my fate for the next four years.**

The **only** thing that **consoled** me?

The **only** difference between my school and this college? **Phones were allowed.** And we had **IV tours.**

That's it. Nothing else. No big change, no freedom, just these two things.

And so, with a phone in my hand and IV tours to look forward to, I stepped into this so-called *college life,* knowing deep down that it wasn't the dream I had imagined.

THE FIRST-YEAR TALE

I walked into my classroom, sitting cluelessly, unsure of what to expect.

It was August 28th—just a day after my birthday. I had barely gotten over the excitement of turning 17, and now, here I was, stepping into an entirely new phase of life. College.

Unlike school, there were no strict rules about uniforms on the first day, so I walked in wearing casual clothes, feeling both nervous and out of place. Everyone around me was a stranger, and the idea of spending four years in this environment felt overwhelming.

My dad had already sealed my fate by choosing this college for me. It was far from home, old-fashioned, and completely void of any fun or culturals. The only relief? I wasn't alone.

One familiar face was waiting for me—my dad's friend's daughter—Susmitha. She knew me, but I barely knew her.

And thanks to my dad's recommendation, she ended up in the same college as me. Her fate changed because of me, haha! At least I had someone to sit with on the first day.

As I sat there, unfamiliar faces started filling the room, one by one. Some looked nervous, some excited, and others completely unbothered. I just observed, trying to guess who would be the troublemakers, the nerds, and the teacher's pets.

Then came the staff introductions. Professors walked in one after another, introducing themselves, explaining the college rules, and emphasizing how phones were strictly prohibited inside the classroom. (*Yeah, right! We still managed to use them.*)

And, of course, the one thing that never changes from school to college—self-introductions. Just like in school, we had to stand up and say our name, background, and something about ourselves. I was already bored.

But what I really loved? The window seat. Sitting there, I had the perfect view of students walking freely outside, skipping classes like it was no big deal.

Sometimes, I'd watch them and wonder what it felt like to be that carefree, but at the same time, I found comfort in my little corner.

Somehow, wherever I go, I always manage to find a good spot—heehee!

Lucky them! Meanwhile, I was stuck inside, forced to listen to never-ending lectures on rules and regulations.

Then, something completely unexpected happened.

One day, while I was sitting in class, two of my schoolmates, Dhani and Vaish, suddenly walked in. I was fully surprised! I had no idea they had joined the same college as me.

Back in school, we were part of different groups, but still, it felt good to see familiar faces in a new place.

Seeing familiar faces in a place where I thought I knew no one felt like a weird but welcome coincidence. It instantly made me feel a little more at ease.

AND THEN, THERE WAS GULNAZ.

Fate has a weird sense of humor. Some friendships start with a smile, some with a random conversation, and some… well, some start in the middle of a chaotic, overcrowded bus ride.

Mine with Gulnaz? It started with a simple act—offering her my seat.

That day, I was lucky enough to grab the front single seat, comfortably sitting while vibing to my playlist, completely unaware that destiny had other plans.

Meanwhile, Gulnaz was standing, struggling to keep her balance, gripping onto the handle as if her life depended on it. The bus was packed, and she looked like she was in the final round of a survival game—if she let go, she was gone.

As the stops passed, the bus started emptying, and soon, she was the only one still standing. I glanced at her, noticing how she kept shifting her weight from one foot to another, clearly tired but too stubborn to ask for a seat. Something about that made me chuckle.

Without a second thought, I stood up and gestured for her to sit. She blinked at me, surprised, as if she wasn't sure whether to accept or argue. But before she could protest, I had already moved to the opposite seat.

The bus started moving again, and that's when I noticed her struggling. She was trying to balance herself, but every time the bus jerked, she wobbled like a toddler learning to walk.

I sighed, stretched my hand out, and without thinking much, held onto hers to steady her. "Just sit properly," I said, pulling her down into the seat.

She looked at me with wide eyes—probably wondering if this was some hidden-camera prank. But instead of questioning it, she just sat.

And that was it—the start of an unexpected, chaotic, and totally vibe-matching friendship.

And let me tell you, Gulnaz? She wasn't just any random girl. She was a walking paradox—innocent as a baby deer but with a wild energy that could match mine.

We clicked instantly, like long-lost troublemakers finally reunited. From that day on, our conversations went from "Hi" to "Bro, let's do something crazy today."

And guess what? We always did.

Escaping the Ordinary

As days passed, I slowly started figuring out ways to escape the routine. Sitting through boring lectures all day? Not happening.

I became an expert at making up excuses—sometimes I'd say I needed to go to the library, other times I'd pretend I had some urgent work at the office.

But in reality? I'd just escape to the canteen or take a long walk around the campus, enjoying a break from the dullness of the classroom.

At first, even the staff members seemed dull, especially one professor who looked *way* too strict. I was convinced he'd be one of those lecturers who were all about rules, assignments, and no fun. But over time, I realized he was different.

He wasn't just there to teach and leave—he actually cared. He made sure we understood, asked if we were struggling, and even remembered small details about us. If someone was falling behind, he'd help instead of just scolding them. *That* was unexpected.

I guess first impressions aren't always right. The professor I assumed would be the strictest turned out to be one of the best. And that's rare to find.

The Moment Everyone Knew Me

The first few days of college were slow, routine, and mostly uneventful. I kept to myself, attending classes, sitting by the window, and observing everything around me. But then, **one incident changed everything.**

It all started with a **math problem** in our class group. One of the boys had sent a solution, but there was something **wrong with it**. I simply asked him to **check it again**, but instead of correcting his mistake, he replied,

"If you know everything, then do it on your own."

That was it. **I lost it.**

Without thinking twice, I **stood up in the middle of the class** and shouted, **"Who the hell just said that?"**

The entire classroom went **silent**. Heads turned. People who hadn't even noticed me before were now staring. Some looked amused, some were shocked, and some were just waiting for drama to unfold. The boy who made the comment didn't say a word after that.

And just like that, **everyone in the class knew who I was.**

The So-Called "Events"

Every time the college announces an event, there's a brief moment of excitement, a tiny hope that maybe—just maybe—this time, it will be different. But reality hits hard.

The so-called "event" usually means sitting in an auditorium, staring at a stage where people give long, monotonous speeches.

No energy, no enthusiasm, just a painfully slow passage of time. Even if something remotely interesting is planned, it gets wrapped up in restrictions—no loud cheering, no fun, just a neatly controlled environment where excitement is practically banned.

Sometimes, there's a competition, but participation is either forced or discouraged. And if someone dares to actually enjoy it?

The fun is shut down before it even begins. It's like they believe students are here only to exist, not to experience anything beyond the textbooks.

But then, there's the symposium—the one event that actually feels like an escape. Not because of what happens inside, but because we get OD (On Duty) and the freedom to roam around without being stuck in class.

Whether we participate or not doesn't even matter. The real fun is in wandering freely, chilling with friends, and for once, feeling like college isn't just about rules and routines.

At this point, whenever an event is announced, I don't even bother asking what it is. Because in this place, "event" is just another word for wasting time in a different way—except for symposiums, the only time we actually get a taste of freedom.

While We Scrolled, They Built

There will always be students in class who make us rethink how we spend our time—those who remind us that while we're lost in an endless scroll of reels, time is slipping through our fingers. In our class, Harish and Nafeed were those students. They weren't just focused; they were unstoppable.

While we wasted hours talking about things that didn't matter, they were busy chasing their goals. Harish never cared about what others thought—he had a vision, and he followed it with quiet determination.

Nafeed, on the other hand, had this intense energy, always pushing himself forward, never letting setbacks slow him down. They weren't the ones sitting in the library or staring at their screens—they were out there, doing the work, making things happen in real time.

There's one thing that made me admire **Nafeed**—his patience. No matter how chaotic things got, he never rushed, never panicked.

While everyone else was losing their minds over instant results, he just stayed calm, did his thing, and trusted the process. And you know what? It always worked in his favor.

Life didn't make it easy for them. There were moments when things didn't go their way, when the path they had chosen felt like an uphill battle.

But even then, they never let failure define them. I saw them struggle, but I also saw them rise, again and again, refusing to give in.

And somehow, I feel glad that I was there, witnessing their journey—not just in their victories but also in their lowest moments. Because now, when I look at them, I see proof that hard work pays off. That passion and persistence win over distractions.

Most of us are still figuring out where we're headed, still caught between dreams and procrastination. But Harish and Nafeed? They're already on their way, proving that those who stay focused are the ones who truly move forward.

They didn't waste time chasing trends or scrolling through endless reels like the rest of us. They were always working on something—something big, something nobody quite understood yet. When they entered the class, they didn't try to impress anyone. And yet, everyone noticed them.

THE POWER OF PATIENCE

The reason for their success? Patience.

The biggest problem with us? We have zero patience. We live in a world that thrives on speed—fast results, Their reason for their success? Patience.

While the world rushes toward instant gratification, the truly successful understand that great things take time. They plant seeds and nurture them, knowing that growth is a process, not an event.

The richest, the strongest, the wisest—they all have one thing in common: they waited, they worked, and they endured.

We want instant replies, instant fixes, instant happiness. And the moment things take time, we panic. We get frustrated. We start doubting ourselves.

But here's the truth: the strongest people aren't the fastest—they're the most patient. They know that anything worth having takes time.

They understand that growth happens in silence, that power is built in the waiting, that the ones who hold their ground always win in the end.

Think about it. Nature never rushes, yet everything falls into place perfectly. A tree doesn't fight to grow faster—it just keeps standing, letting the seasons do their work.

A river doesn't force its flow—it carves its path slowly, shaping the earth itself. And a caterpillar? It doesn't break out of its cocoon before time—it waits. It struggles. It transforms.

That's the secret. Patience isn't a weakness—it's a superpower. The moment you master it, you become untouchable. No rejection can shake you. No failure can break you.

No delay can make you desperate. Because you know your time is coming, and when it does, you'll be ready.

How many times have you rushed into something and regretted it later? How many wrong people have you entertained because you didn't have the patience to wait for the right ones?

How many dreams have you given up on just because results weren't instant? We destroy our own blessings because we don't trust the process.

We force things that aren't meant for us, and then cry when they break. We chase people who don't deserve us, and then wonder why we feel empty. We settle for less when patience could've given us everything.

Once you learn patience, you become dangerous. You stop begging for attention, stop getting frustrated over delays, stop doubting yourself over setbacks.

Instead, you move with silent confidence. You know that what's meant for you is already on its way. You stop running after things that don't align with you. You start trusting that the universe isn't ignoring you—it's preparing you.

So, let the world rush. Let them stress. Let them break themselves trying to force what isn't ready. You? You'll wait. You'll grind. You'll grow. And when your moment comes, you won't just take it—you'll own it.

WHEN NO BECOMES POWER

The biggest lesson I learned in my first year of college was simple yet powerful—*if it's a no, say a strong no.* No hesitation, no second thoughts, no guilt.

And this isn't just about love. It's about everything in life.

If you don't want to do something, say no. If you're uncomfortable, say no. If something doesn't feel right, say no. It doesn't matter who is asking—whether it's a friend, a teacher, a senior, or even family.

Your choices are yours alone, and no one should force you into something you don't want.

But here's something just as important—*don't expect everyone to respect your "no."*

There will always be people who try to manipulate, guilt-trip, or pressure you. They'll make you feel like saying no is wrong, that you owe them something. But here's the truth: *you don't.* You don't owe anyone your peace, your comfort, or your choices.

It's Not Just About Saying No, It's About Standing By It

Saying no is easy. Sticking to it is the hard part. People will push, beg, or even threaten. They'll test your limits just to see if you'll bend.

But once you give in, even once, they'll know they can break you again. And that's why a *no* should always mean *no*, without conditions, without explanations, without doubt.

Guilt is Not a Reason to Say Yes

Sometimes, we say yes just because we don't want to hurt someone. We think, *What if they feel bad? What if they hate me?*

But saying yes out of guilt is the easiest way to lose yourself. If someone truly cares about you, they will respect your choices, even if they don't like them. And if they don't, then they never truly cared in the first place.

Choosing Yourself is Not Selfish

Many times, we hesitate to say no because we're afraid of being called selfish. But choosing yourself is not selfish—it's necessary.

You cannot pour from an empty cup. You cannot live your life constantly trying to please others while sacrificing your own happiness.

At the end of the day, your life is yours to live. Not theirs. Not anyone else's. So when the moment comes, and you feel the pressure to say yes when your heart screams no—remember this: *Your voice matters. Your choices matter. And you deserve to be heard.*

The power of saying no was the first and most important thing I learned in my first year.

First Year Chronicles

People always say, *"Once you finish school, college life will be fun!"* But let me tell you, that's the biggest scam I've ever fallen for. Don't believe those polished words. I did too, and oh, how wrong I was.

I thought college would be my grand escape, a fresh start where I'd finally taste freedom, make unforgettable memories, and live the best years of my life.

But reality? It didn't just slap me—it knocked me out cold.

Looking back, my first year was full of unexpected moments. It wasn't just about lectures and assignments—it was about figuring out how to survive the chaos, making excuses to escape classes, and finding people who made the dull days fun and what truly kept us energized were the IV tours.

From random canteen breaks to last-minute exam cramming, every day had its own little adventure. Some rules were strict, some events were boring, but somewhere in between, there were moments that made it all worth it.

And just like that, the first year ended—not with a grand finale, but with a quiet realization: college life may not have been perfect, but it was definitely unforgettable.

TRAPPED IN THE ROUTINE

Now, in the present, I feel like the first year was much better than this. At least back then, there was some freedom to breathe.

Now? We can't even step out of the classroom except during break time, and the frustration of sitting through boring lectures is at an all-time high.

It's been a year since I joined this college, and I still don't like it. The classroom environment is terrible, the place itself feels lifeless, and the students in my class? They're like Tom and Jerry—constantly at odds, creating chaos, and making it impossible to have a peaceful moment.

Sometimes, it's entertaining to watch, but most of the time, it's just exhausting.

The fun I once imagined college life to be? Nowhere to be found. No culturals, no fests, no excitement—just a robotic routine that repeats every day.

Wake up, go to college, sit through lectures, come back home, and repeat. It feels like living in an endless loop where even the smallest change feels like a big deal.

Most of the lectures don't interest me, so I just manage on my own.

Somehow, I've cleared all my exams so far, and now I'm in my fourth semester, waiting for my third-semester results—

not that I think about them much. We almost forget about results until they suddenly show up out of nowhere, ready to give us a mini heart attack.

The only thing that keeps me sane is the small moments of relief—random conversations, laughing at something stupid, or just zoning out in class, lost in my own world. At this point, I've mastered the art of looking like I'm paying attention while actually thinking about everything else.

But at the end of the day, it all feels the same. A never-ending loop of dullness.

But there is one thing that excites me—the one place where I can be truly myself, unfiltered and raw. This book.

Here, I can pour out everything, from the tiniest annoyances to the biggest frustrations.

It's the only escape from the monotony, the only thing that feels truly mine in a place where everything else feels forced.

THE GREAT IV WAR

We entered the second year knowing that we could finally go on an IV tour. That one thought was enough to keep us going through all the dull lectures, endless assignments, and the same old routine.

The dream of escaping college for a few days, traveling with friends, and finally experiencing some fun made everything feel a little less suffocating.

Slowly, the discussions about the IV started taking place— where to go, how to convince the faculty, and, of course, the endless debates over dates and budgets.

The plan? Simple. Gather 40+ students, finalize the list, and go. The reality? Absolute *chaos*.

Let me tell you, handling my girls was a piece of cake. We sorted out our list in a day—quick discussions, no unnecessary drama, just straight to the point.

But the boys? Oh lord. If I thought they lacked unity before, this IV planning proved that they were *genetically programmed to create problems.*

One moment, someone was in. The next moment, *"Bro, I don't think I can come."* Then another genius would come up with a new reason—*"What if the weather isn't good?"* Excuse me? We were going to Ooty, not Antarctica.

And then there was that one guy who said, *"I'll come if my best friend comes."* Like, dude, are we in kindergarten? Do you need someone to hold your hand while you pee too?

Days passed, and the list was still not finalized. And that's when I snapped. I had been watching the circus unfold for too long, and now it was time to step in.

I gathered everyone, took a deep breath, and declared, "Listen up, everyone. We are GOING. No matter who comes or who doesn't, the ones who gave their names are expected to show up.

No excuses. If you're not coming, just give us the money and stay at home. We've been waiting long enough, and it's time to get this done. Either you're in, or you're out.

I spoke with the confidence of a mafia boss delivering an ultimatum, and trust me, it worked. The final list was set. The date was fixed. But just when I thought *finally, some peace*—life decided to play one last cruel joke.

The other department who had planned the same IV as us? Their bus arrived EARLY. Meanwhile, ours? It showed up at 12 AM. Let me repeat: TWELVE. MIDNIGHT. After we had already been waiting for HOURS. By the time the bus rolled in, my brain was already halfway to hell and back. Mind-fuck wasn't even the right word to describe the exhaustion.

And then the journey began. And let me tell you, the bus ride? THAT was the actual vacation. Singing, dancing, screaming song lyrics at the top of our lungs—it was pure madness. The kind of fun that makes you forget you even had an exhausting day.

But what made it even more special? That day was my friend Subha's birthday. None of us expected it to turn out the way it did, but we all sang for her, making sure it became a memory she'd never forget. And honestly? Neither would I.

But the actual IV? Biggest scam of my life. Some well-meaning authorities made sure we were constantly reminded of the rules and limits.

Don't go there. Don't laugh too much. Don't have fun.

Like, excuse me, am I on a trip or a meditation retreat? If I had known this was going to be a *silent retreat*, I would have just stayed home and slept.

But whatever. The trip wasn't about the place—it was about *who* we were with. And even if it was a struggle, the memories we created? Worth it. But next time? Oh, next time, **I AM CHOOSING THE BUS.**

ALONE IN A CROWD

After all the madness, chaos, and struggle of planning the IV trip, after all the late-night dance sessions on the bus and the adrenaline of finally making it happen, everything came back to normal.

The usual routine, the same old faces, the same college hallways. But something felt different. Or maybe, it was just me.

College life is supposed to be a mix of fun, friendships, and memories that last a lifetime. But what happens when the people you call friends hesitate when you need them the most?

I have three friends. Each of them is different in their own way. Two of them are kind and caring but always hesitate when it comes to standing up for me.

They avoid problems, always worrying about what others might think. And the third? She's always busy on her phone, lost in a world that doesn't include me.

At first, I ignored it. Maybe I was overthinking. Maybe I was expecting too much. But then, there was one incident that I could never forget.

But at the same time, I know my friends tried. In their own way, they made efforts to keep me included, to make me feel like I belonged—even if they didn't always get it right. And maybe, that's what truly matters.

One day, on my way home in the college van, I got into a small argument with someone. It wasn't anything serious, just a heated exchange of words.

But in that moment, I realized something—when it came to standing by my side, my friends disappeared. One of them was on leave that day, but the other was sitting right there, a few feet away.

She knew exactly what was happening. She saw everything. And yet, she didn't move. She just sat in her seat, watching, silent.

I was used to fighting my own battles, but this time, it hit differently. Because if I were in her place, I wouldn't have hesitated. I would have stood for her without a second thought.

That's what friends do. But when it was my turn, she just stayed back, as if it had nothing to do with her.

When I reached my stop, my mom saw me and immediately sensed something was wrong. She scolded me—not for arguing, but for standing alone. She saw what my friend failed to see.

That night, my friend texted me. Just one word:

"Sorry."

A simple word, but it didn't change what had already happened.

Time passed, and I told myself to forget about it. But sometimes, when I sit in silence, the thought creeps back into my mind. I have friends, yet I feel alone.

Maybe it's not about how many people are around you, but whether they truly stand with you when it matters.

Stand Alone, Stand Strong

If you've ever found yourself standing alone in a moment when you needed your friends the most, know this—you are not weak for feeling hurt.

You are not wrong for expecting support. And most importantly, you are not alone in this feeling.

Friendship isn't about just having people around; it's about having people who stand with you, even in uncomfortable situations.

If your friends hesitate when you need them, if they stay silent when you're fighting alone, then ask yourself—are they really the right people for you?

You don't need a crowd to feel valued. Even one true friend who stands by you is better than a hundred who stay back and watch. And if you don't have that person yet, **be your own strength** until you find them.

Never beg for loyalty, never ask for support that should come naturally. **And most importantly, never lower your voice just because no one is speaking up with you.** Stand tall, stand strong, and trust that one day, you will find people who match your energy, who won't think twice before standing with you.

Until then, **be your own hero.**

The Convenience of Friendship

I've seen it happen so many times—people who act like they care, but only when they need something. They appear out of nowhere, all friendly and sweet, but the moment they get what they want, they disappear as if you never existed.

And the worst part? They don't even realize how obvious they are. It's frustrating, isn't it? To be treated like an option, like a tool that's picked up when needed and tossed aside when not.

I tried ignoring it, convincing myself that maybe I was overthinking. But no matter how many times I let it slide, the cycle kept repeating.

Someone would ask for help, I'd help them, and then they'd walk away without a second thought. And then, days or weeks later, they'd come back as if nothing had happened, acting like we were close.

And let's not forget those people who only keep other people around because they can't stand being alone. What's that about? I've seen people just be "friends" with others because they feel the need to have someone there.

But, bro, that's not friendship, that's just filling a void. It's wrong. When you need company so badly that you're willing to hang out with anyone, even if there's no real connection, it just feels fake.

With time, I learned that not everyone who talks to you is your friend. Some people are just there for their own benefit, and it's okay to recognize that. I stopped feeling bad about it.

Instead of getting upset, I started observing. I noticed how they only showed up when they needed notes, assignments, or some kind of favor.

I noticed how conversations with them always had a purpose—never just to check in, never just to talk. And I realized that I didn't have to entertain such one-sided connections.

So I started drawing my boundaries. I stopped saying yes to everyone. If someone only came to me when they needed something, I didn't hesitate to say no.

It wasn't easy at first—I was so used to helping people that saying no felt unnatural. But slowly, it became clear that I wasn't losing anything by doing so. Instead, I was saving my time and energy for people who actually valued me, not just what I could offer.

The truth is, we all deserve friends who stay, even when they don't need anything from us. Friends who check in, who remember the small things, who are there simply because they want to be, not because they need a favor.

And once you recognize the difference between real friends and the ones who only show up when it benefits them, life becomes a lot easier.

Beyond Friendship

Friendship, just like love, is one of the basic human needs that we all seek—someone to confide in, share moments with, and grow alongside. But there's a difference in how we approach it, especially when we're young.

As we navigate through life, it's easy to form friendships out of convenience, just because we don't want to be alone or because we feel like we need to fit in. But true friendship goes beyond just being around for the sake of having company.

It's about being there for each other, understanding each other, and supporting one another, not because you need something from the other person, but because you genuinely value them.

Now, this concept extends to love. At a young age, it's easy to mistake infatuation or the need for companionship for true love. You're still learning, still figuring out what you really need and want in a relationship.

And just like with friendships, it's important to take a step back and think about whether your feelings are truly genuine or just driven by the convenience of being in a relationship.

It took me a long time to understand that real love isn't about rushing into something just because it feels right in the moment. It's about knowing yourself, understanding your emotions, and realizing that sometimes, it's okay to let go.

When you're under 18, you're still discovering what it means to truly connect with someone in a deep, meaningful way, and it's important to give yourself the time and space to grow.

Sometimes, it's easy to fall into a relationship because you're used to the comfort of companionship, but real love comes when you're ready—not out of convenience.

So, just like with friendship, don't force love. If it happens, it happens, and it will be for the right reasons. And remember, no matter how much you might think you've found the one at a young age, you have a whole life ahead of you.

Don't rush; don't hurt others in the process. Focus on growing, on being a better friend, a better person, and, when the time is right, love will come naturally.

When Love Turns to Possession

It always began so innocently. At first, it was just his constant presence—like a shadow that followed wherever you went. The way he lingered in your thoughts, the way he made sure you knew he was there, every minute of the day.

It felt comforting at first, like you were the center of his world, like you mattered in ways that no one else did. His eyes would light up every time you entered the room, and his words would wrap around you like a warm blanket.

He was protective, attentive, and you couldn't help but feel special.

But somewhere along the way, the warmth turned cold, and that comfort began to suffocate.

It started with small things—little comments here and there. "I don't like how much time you spend with him," he'd say, his voice low but firm, as if it was somehow wrong for you to talk to someone outside of him.

He'd joke about how you should "stay close" to him, not letting anyone else get too comfortable in your space.

At first, you thought it was cute, like he just wanted to make sure no one took you away. But the jokes stopped being funny when they began to feel more like rules.

He wasn't asking for your time anymore; he was demanding it. He wanted to know where you were, who you were with, and how long you'd be gone. Every minute you spent away from him felt like a betrayal, as if you owed him your every second.

The constant check-ins became more frequent, and his need to keep you in his orbit became an unspoken rule of the relationship. You didn't question it at first.

After all, he was just looking out for you, right? He was just showing how much he cared.

But possessiveness had a way of creeping in unnoticed. It wasn't the kind of love that made you feel free or valued— it was the kind that twisted affection into something else, something darker.

It wasn't enough to simply care about you. He wanted to own you, to control the spaces you moved in, to claim the moments you shared with others.

He started to make you feel guilty for having your own life, for not always being available, for giving anyone else your attention.

His love became a demand, an expectation. He wasn't just afraid of losing you—he was terrified of sharing you.

But the line between love and control wasn't always clear. As his possessiveness deepened, so did his need to dictate everything about your life.

He started to voice opinions on things you never imagined would be up for debate—what you wore, where you went, who you spent time with. "You shouldn't wear that," he would say, as though his opinion was the only one that mattered.

"Why are you still friends with her? She's not good for you."

At first, it felt like a concern. He was protecting you, right? He was just looking out for your well-being, ensuring that you stayed safe, that you didn't get hurt.

But the more he spoke, the more you realized that he wasn't just concerned for you—he was shaping you into the person he needed you to be. He wasn't asking for your opinion; he was commanding it. He didn't just want your company—he wanted you to be his, in every way.

And somewhere between the constant surveillance, the criticisms, and the subtle demands, you began to question yourself.

The things you used to enjoy, the friends you used to love, the places you used to go—they all started to feel wrong. Not because they were, but because he made you believe they were.

He wasn't just controlling your actions; he was controlling your thoughts, your sense of self.

What was the difference, you might wonder? Possessiveness might make you feel wanted, desired, but controlling behavior makes you feel like a puppet, with every string pulled by someone else. Possessiveness came from insecurity, a fear of losing you. But controlling? Controlling was a weapon.

It wasn't about caring for you—it was about owning you. It wasn't about love; it was about power.

And the worst part? You didn't even realize it was happening. You didn't see the walls closing in until you were already trapped.

But there was something powerful in that realization. A moment when the scales finally fell from your eyes, and you saw it for what it was—an unhealthy need to control, disguised as love. And once you saw the difference, you couldn't unsee it.

Love shouldn't feel like a cage. It shouldn't feel like a constant test of loyalty, a game of who can hold on tighter. Love should make you feel like you can breathe, like you can grow, like you can be yourself, unapologetically.

When someone's love makes you feel like you're drowning, it's time to recognize the difference. When love becomes ownership, it's no longer love—it's a prison.

And the only way to escape is to break free, to reclaim your own breath and your own space.

Be Loved for Who You Are, Not Who They Want You to Be

Love is a beautiful thing, but only when it allows you to remain who you are. It's natural to adjust, to compromise, to grow alongside someone—but the moment love asks you to shrink, to erase parts of yourself just to fit into someone else's world, it is no longer love.

True love never demands that you become someone you're not. It never forces you to silence your dreams, change your identity, or lose your spark just to make the other person comfortable. The right love will never feel like a battle between who you are and who they want you to be.

Yes, relationships require effort, understanding, and sometimes change. But those changes should be a result of growth, not sacrifice.

The right person will love you for the way you laugh, the way you dream, the way you exist—not for the version of you they can control.

Love should feel like home, not a battlefield where you have to fight for the right to be yourself. It's natural to grow together, to make small adjustments, to learn from each other—but if someone asks you to abandon who you are, that's not love. That's control wrapped in pretty words.

If love is real, it marries you for who you are now—not for some version they hope to mold you into. If they truly love you, they won't ask you to erase your beliefs, your identity, or your essence just to fit their expectations. Love should never come with conditions that make you lose yourself.

And if they ask you to change your faith, your values, or your soul just to be with them—run. Run, and don't look back. Because love that demands your sacrifice isn't love. It's a cage. And the moment you step inside, you may never fully escape.

Love doesn't require losing yourself. The right person will hold your hand and walk beside you, not ask you to walk away from yourself. Adapt, yes. Grow, yes. But never let love strip you of the person you were always meant to be.

A NEW YEAR, A NEW SCAR

Love may or may not become your lifelong journey. Some might have experienced what love truly is, and I thought I had too. I had one—what I believed to be a love that would last forever. But it ended in betrayal.

The new year arrived, bringing with it a storm that shattered everything I thought I understood about love and trust.

My first year had ended, leaving behind memories, lessons, and people I had outgrown. With a new mindset, I entered my second year, determined to leave the past behind and focus on the present.

But life had other plans for me.

It was just a regular day, or so I thought. The day before, everything had seemed fine. I went to a movie with her.

We laughed, shared snacks, and talked about anything and everything, just like we always did. There was no indication of what was coming. She didn't say a word. She sat next to me, knowing the truth, yet chose silence.

And then, the next day, I got a call—not from her, but from him. "I thought you should know... I'm with her now."

For a moment, I thought I misheard him. My brain refused to process the words, but the silence that followed, the weight behind them, made it all too real.

Her. My best friend. The one I trusted enough to introduce to him. The one who had been by my side for seven years. And now she was with the person I once loved.

I had so many questions, but the biggest one was: Why didn't she tell me? Why didn't she show me the respect I thought we shared?

When I confronted her, I didn't yell or accuse. I just wanted to understand. "Why didn't you tell me?"

She hesitated, apologized, and said she didn't know how to bring it up. She confessed it had been going on for a while. And then, she said the words that shattered me— "One night… I went in his car."

At that moment, everything crashed down on me. Betrayal, anger, sadness—everything at once. But what broke me more wasn't the betrayal itself—it was her reaction.

"I didn't do anything wrong!" she said, as if she was the one being unfairly accused. "I didn't plan for this to happen! It just happened!"

Just happened. As if it wasn't a choice.

What hurt the most wasn't even the betrayal. It was how she acted afterward. Her replies grew cold, her attitude shifted. The warmth that once defined our friendship was gone. She made the mistake, but I was the one being pushed away.

The day before, we had shared a laugh, a movie—everything seemed fine. And the very next day, she casually told me the truth, as if it was no big deal.

Seven years of friendship—gone in an instant.

And that's when I truly understood—sometimes, it's not the breakups that hurt the most. It's the friendships that end without a proper goodbye.

Maybe I deserve this. Maybe it was a consequence of the hurt I had caused someone else in the past. After all, life has a way of balancing things out, right?

It could be that what I experienced was the universe's way of making me pay for my own mistakes.

It's funny how we tend to forget the times we've hurt others when we're on the receiving end of pain.

Maybe I took some relationships for granted, maybe I didn't treat some people the way they deserved, and now, here I was—on the other side of that feeling. But even then, knowing that doesn't make it any easier to swallow.

I don't know if I'll ever understand why she did what she did, but deep down, part of me couldn't help but wonder if this was just a reminder to be more careful with people's hearts. It's a painful realization, but it's also a lesson—one I'll carry with me.

THE SCENT OF MEMORIES

That smell—it's the only thing I have left, the one connection to everything that once was. It's strange how something as simple as a scent can hold so many memories, so many moments that now feel like they belong to another time, another place.

He had returned everything, all the things that meant something to us. But there was one thing he said was lost, the one thing I had given him—my favorite perfume.

It's odd, isn't it? How something so small can linger in your mind, long after everything else has faded. I often wonder if he remembers it the same way, or if it's just another piece of the past he's tucked away, just like everything else.

It's hard to let go, especially when the memories are all you're left with. The smell still takes me back to moments that now seem so distant, like flashes of something that should've lasted longer.

I don't know if he ever thinks of them too—those moments we had, the little things that seemed like they meant something at the time.

And yet, it's in that smell, the faint trace that lingers in the air, that I find myself holding on. Maybe it's just the last thread I have to what was.

That perfume, the one he said was lost, is the only reminder I have of him now. Sometimes, when I close my eyes, I can still imagine it, feel it—like I'm back in those moments, when everything felt right.

It's funny how such a small thing could carry so much weight. But maybe that's all it is.

The things we leave behind—sometimes, it's not the big gestures, but the smallest details that stay with us. And even if it's only a scent now, it's enough. It's enough to remind me of what once was and what I had hoped could last forever, even if it didn't.

In a way, that smell is all I have left, and in a strange sense, it's all I need. Because as long as it lingers, I'll have a piece of what we once shared.

Even if the rest fades away, the scent, the memories, they remain—faint, but enough to remind me of what I had and what I lost.

Maybe that's how it's meant to be—small, subtle, yet carrying a weight that nothing else could.

The power of scent is truly astonishing. One splash of a fragrance, especially one tied to a significant memory, can instantly change your mood.

It's like the fragrance has the ability to pull you back in time, right to that specific moment when that person or memory was a part of your life.

The smell triggers a flood of emotions, whether it's warmth, happiness, or even sadness.

It can feel like your whole world shifts for a second, as the memory becomes so real and vivid in that moment.

It's a double-edged sword, really. On one hand, the scent can bring back beautiful memories—those moments when everything felt right.

But on the other hand, if that memory is tied to a person or an experience that hurt you, it can bring up feelings of loss or betrayal, like you're living through it all over again.

It's crazy how something as simple as a fragrance can have such an emotional impact, right?

"I truly believe that scent is one of the most precious gifts a person could give to another, especially if it's the exact perfume they wear. There's something about the personal connection to it, like giving a piece of yourself that lingers in the air long after you're gone. A fragrance can carry memories, emotions, and even the essence of a person, all wrapped up in a single, fleeting moment."

WHEN KINDNESS IS MISUNDERSTOOD

The people who once spoke sweet words, the ones I trusted and confided in, have now become the ones I hate the most. It's crazy how life can twist everything around, turning love into betrayal and friendship into something toxic.

I never thought it would be these same people who'd shatter everything I believed in.

I always believed in treating people with kindness, offering my warmth without hesitation. But what I didn't realize was how easily that kindness could be mistaken for weakness. I showed care, and they twisted it into something ugly.

The people I laughed with, shared my life with, turned into strangers who whispered behind my back, spreading rumors and lies about me. It didn't make sense. How could the people I trusted the most betray me so easily?

The most painful part wasn't even the lies or the rumors—it was when someone I deeply loved revealed the truth.

It wasn't the words that hurt the most; it was the realization that the people I stood by, the ones I fought for, never stood by me in return.

Some people are masters of acting—hurting you in silence, betraying you without remorse, and then walking right past you as if nothing happened.

But what shocked me even more was how easily they pretended. The same people who had been talking behind my back would show up, chatting like we were the best of friends, with no shame, no guilt.

It was almost impressive how effortlessly they faked it. But I wasn't impressed. I saw through it.

That's when I learned the art of pretending—not for them, but for myself. I didn't have to expose their lies or wear my pain on my sleeve. Instead, I became indifferent.

I realized that all the energy I was wasting trying to prove my truth to people who didn't deserve it was pointless. The moment I stopped explaining myself, I won.

But then I understood something. They were the ones who should feel ashamed—not me. Because I know my worth. I'm not defined by their assumptions or their betrayal.

My kindness is not weakness, and my silence is not acceptance. I'm done letting these people back in.

And let me tell you something, you ugly creatures who think you can hide behind your lies and pretend like nothing happened: **You will suffer for what you've done. This isn't a curse, it's a promise.**

You think you've gotten away with it, but you haven't.

The universe has a way of making you pay for the pain you've caused. Don't forget—karma has its way of finding you.

If you've got the guts to talk behind my back, then why not come in front and say it straight to my face? Don't hide behind whispers or fake smiles. Be real. Own it.

Don't expect me to pretend I don't see through you, because I do. I'm done with people who can't even face the consequences of their actions.

So, to anyone out there feeling betrayed or misunderstood—remember this: Their actions speak volumes about them, and nothing about you.

Let them act. Let them pretend. But never let them make you forget who you are.

Try to be kind to others, but never let that kindness be taken for granted.

Walk in My Shoes Before You Judge

People see me and think I have everything. They see my confidence, my strength, the way I walk and talk like nothing can break me. They assume I have no struggles, no worries, no pain.

But what they don't see are the silent battles I fought, the nights I cried with no one to wipe my tears, and the scars I carry that no one even notices.

I used to trust too easily. I believed in love, in promises, in forever. But life had other plans. **I was betrayed. Broken. Lied to.** And the worst part? The ones who hurt me never looked back.

They moved on like nothing happened, while I spent sleepless nights trying to understand why.

But here's what I realized—**I don't need their answers anymore.** I don't need closure from people who never valued me.

I don't need apologies from those who never meant their promises in the first place. What I need is **myself.** My dreams. My peace. And my own strength.

So, I stopped expecting. I stopped waiting for people to change. I stopped letting their words and actions control my happiness. Now, I live for myself.

Not for society, not for love, not for anyone who once walked away. **I live on my own terms.**

Yes, I have an attitude. **But if you think it's arrogance, you're wrong.** This attitude? It comes from everything I've survived. From the pain I've turned into power.

From the betrayals that made me fearless. I am not cold-hearted—I just refuse to be played again. **So don't judge me unless you've lived my life.** Before you speak about me, ask yourself—**do you really know my story?**

I will build my own success. I will find peace away from toxic people. I will have a life where I don't have to depend on anyone, where I wake up every day doing something I love, and where no one can break me again.

I won't let my past define me. Instead, I'll let it fuel me. **I will rise, stronger than ever, and one day, I'll look back and thank myself for never giving up.**

People love to pretend they are righteous. They fast, they pray, they show the world how "pure" they are. But what's the point of all that if your heart is filled with hatred? If your words destroy someone instead of lifting them?

Religion, rituals, and traditions mean nothing if your character is rotten.

So before you preach goodness, **be good first.** Before you talk about faith, **have a heart that understands humanity.** Before you try to break someone, **ask yourself if you would survive the same pain.**

Behave like a human first. Keep your heart clean before you try to prove yourself holy. Because at the end of the day, it's not what you show the world that matters—it's what's truly inside you.

Everyone has only one life. **Live it the way you want.** Chase your dreams, love fearlessly, and be true to yourself. But remember—**your happiness should never come at the cost of someone else's pain.**

Don't be the reason for someone's sleepless nights. Don't be the cause of someone's silent tears. Words can heal, but they can also destroy.

A moment of selfishness, a careless betrayal, or a thoughtless rumor can leave scars that never fade. **What do you gain by breaking someone?**

If you want peace in your life, start by giving it to others. If you want happiness, don't steal it from someone else. **Be real. Be kind. And if you can't bring light, at least don't bring darkness.**

Because in the end, life is too short to live with regrets. **So live, but don't hurt. Love, but don't betray. And if you can't help, at least don't harm.**

A Pain Beyond Words

I still remember that day when my friend called me and made me think about how cruel some people can truly be. It was late at night, and the moment I picked up, I could hear her sobbing on the other end.

For a second, I didn't know what to say. I just held the phone close to my ear, listening to her broken cries.

I could feel her pain through the silence between her gasps, through the way her breath trembled as she tried to speak.

"Tell me what happened," I finally whispered.

And then, through the sound of her shattered voice, she told me everything.

She had been in a relationship—a love she thought was real, a love she thought would last. It started off beautifully. He was caring, attentive, and made her feel special in ways no one ever had.

He'd call her just to hear her voice, send her messages filled with sweet promises, and make her believe that she was the only one for him.

Naseer made love sound like forever, like destiny itself had written their names together. But in the end, his words were just beautifully crafted lies, meant to keep her trapped in an illusion he never truly believed in.

She trusted him with everything.

She loved him with everything.

And then, in just a matter of seconds, it all came crashing down.

That day, she had asked him something simple. Just a small, harmless request—"Can you share your phone screen?"

At first, he hesitated. And then, without any warning, he hung up the call.

Minutes later, a message popped up.

"Let's break up."

Just like that. No explanation. No closure. No goodbye.

She didn't understand what was happening. One moment, they were fine, and the next, he was cutting her off like she never mattered.

She tried calling him, but he wouldn't answer.

She sent messages, but he didn't reply.

And then, the truth came out.
He was already with someone else.
Not just recently. From the very beginning.
He had another girl—someone he had loved all along.

When she confronted him, hoping for at least a shred of truth, his response shattered her completely.

"She is my everything. I have loved her from the beginning."

She read those words over and over again, her hands trembling, her chest tightening as if she couldn't breathe.

The man who once promised her forever was now telling her that she was never even a part of his real story.

That night, she felt her world collapse.

Her body refused to function properly. Her fingers wouldn't stop shaking. Her breath felt heavy, as if something was crushing her from the inside. She could barely stand; the pain in her stomach felt like she was being torn apart.

Every heartbeat felt like a wound reopening.

She asked me, "Was I not enough?"

"Was I just a joke to him?"

Her voice cracked with every word.

She had spent months, years, loving someone who had already chosen someone else from the start.

And yet, he didn't even have the decency to let her go gently.

"At least he could have explained… at least he could have said something nice instead of throwing me away like this."

Her words broke me.

How can people be so cruel? How can they play with someone's emotions, knowing damn well they were never planning to stay?

She had done nothing wrong.
She had loved him with everything she had, and yet, she was left feeling like she was the one who lost.

I took a deep breath and told her, "Listen to me."
"You were never the problem. The problem was him—the way he chose dishonesty over honesty, betrayal over loyalty, selfishness over kindness."

"You gave him love, and he gave you lies. And that is his loss, not yours."

"One day, he will look back and realize what he did. Maybe he won't regret losing you, but he will regret never being the kind of man who deserved you in the first place."

"And you? You will heal. You will find love again—real love, not the illusion he fed you."

"But right now, you don't need closure from him. You need to give yourself closure. Don't wait for an apology, don't wait for him to feel guilty. Move forward, because he was never worthy of your time in the first place."

She cried for a while longer, and I just stayed on the phone, letting her feel everything.

Because sometimes, you don't need solutions. You just need someone to remind you that your pain is valid, but it won't last forever.

And in the end, she promised me that she would try.
That she would pick herself up, little by little.
That one day, she would stop looking back.
And I knew, even in her brokenness, that she would.

But let me tell you this—never, ever think that your life should end because of someone who never saw your worth.

It will hurt, of course. It will tear you apart. But one day, all that pain will vanish, and you will experience the kind of love that will make you forget you ever suffered.

A love that will not make you beg for attention.
A love that will not make you question yourself.
A love that will not abandon you in the middle of the night with nothing but heartbreak.

You will smell the scent of true love one day. And when that day comes, you will be grateful that you survived this.

He might have been able to walk away, pretending like nothing happened, laughing with his new girl like nothing ever mattered, his face void of any guilt. But that's on him.

The kind of person he is. He can smile all he wants, but deep down, he knows the truth. And he will have to live with that forever.

In the end, he's the one who will never forget you. And he's the one who will regret what he did.

I told her, "You will rise above this. You will heal and become stronger. One day, when you look back, you'll realize this pain was just a chapter in your story—one that made you who you are now.

And when you find the love you truly deserve, you'll understand why it never worked out with him. He wasn't the one. But you? You're going to be just fine."

Revenge or Karma?

My friend was determined to make him feel the same pain she had experienced. She felt an urge for revenge, for him to understand the weight of his actions. So, she called his so-called girlfriend.

When he found out, he begged her not to, saying that if she ever found out the truth, she would die. But despite his desperate plea, my friend decided to go through with it.

She called the girl, ready to tell her everything. But when she spoke to her, things didn't go as planned.

Instead of spilling the truth, my friend found herself telling a different story—one that wasn't the harsh reality of betrayal but a story that kept her dignity intact. She didn't expose him, didn't let the truth come out, even though it would have been so easy to do so.

When she told me about the call, I could hear the disappointment in her voice. She had expected to tear him down, to make him feel the way she felt, but in the end, she didn't. She didn't drop the bombshell of truth she had been carrying all this time.

Instead, she just let it slip away.

I advised her, "Sometimes, revenge isn't worth the energy.

Let them live their so-called 'happy life'—because deep down, I know they won't be happy for long. Karma's a lot more powerful than any revenge you could get.

It doesn't need you to make it work. In the end, they'll face the consequences of their own actions. And when they do, you won't need to say a word."

She stayed quiet for a moment, and I could feel the weight of it all on her. But then she sighed, as if she understood. "You're right," she whispered.

And just like that, she walked away from it all. She didn't need to tear him down to find peace. Her strength was in letting it go.

While they lived their lie, she was going to live her truth—and that, in itself, was the biggest victory.

Life has a way of throwing people into your path—some to teach you lessons, some to leave scars, and some to remind you of what you should never tolerate again.

And once you've been through enough, you start seeing things differently. **Once you see the real face behind someone's mask, there's no unseeing it.** The way they act, the way they speak—it all starts feeling like a staged performance, a scripted lie.

And that's when a thought hit me so hard, it refused to leave:

Should I take revenge, or should I just let them rot in their own karma?

At first, I won't lie—I wanted revenge. I wanted them to feel the same gut-wrenching pain they put me through.

I wanted them to wake up in the middle of the night, their heart racing, their mind flooded with guilt. I wanted them to taste their own medicine, to realize that the person they once betrayed was not someone to be played with.

And trust me, if I had chosen revenge, I would have done it so **gracefully** that they wouldn't even know what hit them. Because let's be real—when someone underestimates you, the best way to prove them wrong isn't by screaming or begging for an apology.

It's by making them regret ever thinking they could mess with you.

But then I laughed.

Because what's the point? **They weren't worth my energy, my time, or even my hatred.** Taking revenge would mean I still care. And **I don't.** If anything, **I feel sorry for them.** People like that? They don't deserve my anger—they deserve silence.

The real revenge? **It's moving on. It's healing so well that their existence becomes irrelevant to you.**

It's making them watch as you rise, while they stay stuck in the same miserable cycle of their own making. And that? **That hurts them more than anything else ever could.**

And then there's **karma.** Oh, karma never forgets.

I don't need to dirty my hands. Life has a funny way of balancing things out. Maybe not today, maybe not tomorrow, but when the time is right? **Karma will hit them so hard, they'll wish they had never crossed me.** The best part? **I won't even have to lift a finger.**

So, to anyone who has ever been hurt, betrayed, or discarded like they were nothing—**you don't need to do anything.** Don't waste your energy plotting revenge. Don't waste your time waiting for an apology that will never come.

Just sit back, glow up, and **let karma do its job.** Because when it finally strikes? **It never misses.**

The Echo of His Goodbye

My friend— she just wanted to ask one question—just one—because he never answered properly.

Why?

Why did he look at her like she was his world, only to make her feel like a stranger? Why did he hold her so tightly, like he never wanted to let go, only to disappear without a trace? Why did he make her believe in love, forever, if all he meant to give her was an ending?

She trusted him. She gave him her heart, her laughter, her secrets—everything. And if he was always meant to leave, then **why did he kiss her like she was his forever?** Why did he press his forehead against hers, whisper promises he never meant to keep?

His tight hug still lingers in her bones, his scent still clings to her skin like a ghost she can't shake off. Even after he left, it haunts her. The warmth of his arms, the way he made her feel safe—it all keeps hurting her. Because now, she realizes that the safest place she ever knew was nothing but an illusion.

He walked away like she was nothing, but **his presence still refuses to leave.**

And it hurts. **It still hurts.**

But one day, she knows, his scent will fade. His touch will become a memory. The echoes of his voice will grow quieter. And when that day comes, she will finally breathe again.

Without him.

THE WINDOW SEAT ESCAPE

When life fucks you in every direction, spinning you around like you're caught in a cyclone, the only thing that kept me grounded was my daily travel to college. It wasn't just a commute; it was my escape, my moment of peace.

And all of this happened in such a short period of time. One minute, everything was normal. And in the blink of an eye, it felt like my whole world had turned upside down. But every morning, the bus ride was my brief relief from it all.

I'd grab a window seat—my sanctuary—where I could watch the world go by without the weight of everything crashing down on me. The hustle of the streets, the noise, the crowds, they were all just background noise.

I sank into the window seat, pressing my forehead against the cool glass, watching the world blur past.

The day had been overwhelming—anger, sadness, frustration, all tangled inside me like a storm I couldn't calm.

I closed my eyes for a moment, then reached for my earphones. Music—my only escape.

The first song that played was slow, melancholic, the kind that sinks into your soul and makes you feel every hidden wound. As the soft piano melody wrapped around me, my thoughts drifted to everything that had gone wrong.

That's the thing about sad songs—they don't just fill the silence; they make you relive every heartbreak, every regret. But sometimes, that's what you need—to feel it, to let it pass through you instead of burying it.

"Music has the power to heal wounds that medicine cannot touch."

I switched the song. The next one was upbeat, the kind that carried an infectious energy, making my fingers tap against my knee without me even realizing it.

The shift was instant. My heavy heart felt lighter, my mood lifted, and suddenly, I wasn't drowning in thoughts anymore. That's the magic of a good, vibey song—it doesn't ask you to feel better; it just makes you feel it.

"Sometimes, all you need is a song that matches the beat of your heart."

And then, a love song played. One of those soft, dreamy melodies that carried whispers of memories. My fingers hesitated over the screen, but it was too late.

The song had already pulled me in, stirring something deep within me. Suddenly, I found myself staring at the city lights, lost in a wave of nostalgia. Love songs have that power—they can make you miss someone you swore you'd forgotten.

"A song can bring back a thousand memories, even the ones you tried to forget."

As the bus continued moving, I realized how much music had shaped my journey—not just this ride, but my life. It had held me on my worst days, celebrated with me on my best, and reminded me that no feeling was permanent. Every emotion, no matter how strong, would pass—just like a song that fades into the next track.

By the time my stop arrived, I had traveled through emotions I didn't even know I was holding onto. And yet, I felt lighter. Maybe tomorrow will be hard again. Maybe life would throw more storms my way. But as long as there was music, and a window seat to escape into, I knew I would find my way through.

"When words fail, music speaks."

Breaking the Cycle

Enough is enough. No more faking it. No more pretending. No more dragging myself through the mud for people who wouldn't piss on me if I were on fire.

I'm done with the heartbreaks, done with the lies, done with playing small just to make others feel big.

I was always the first to step up. The first to apologize. The first to fix things, even when I had nothing to apologize for.

I'd get stabbed in the back, left hanging on my own, but still, like an idiot, I'd reach out, begging for some sign of care, like a damn fool. Not anymore.

I was sick and tired of being the one who always gave, the one who always cared, the one who kept waiting for people to stop treating me like a backup plan.

No more chasing people who only gave a shit when it was convenient. No more standing there like a sucker, hoping they'd turn around and realize I'm worth the effort. Screw that.

I wasn't going to be the one who always got played. I wasn't going to let people walk all over me, pretending they cared, pretending they had my back, only to turn around and stab me when I wasn't looking. I wasn't going to keep bending over backwards to fix relationships that were already shattered beyond repair.

I was sick of the same damn pattern. I'd step forward, and they'd step back. I'd try to mend things, and they'd let me do all the work. What the hell for? For a fake friendship? For a relationship that was never real in the first place? Hell no. I was done.

I hit rock bottom. But let me tell you, that's when the fire started. That's when I realized I wasn't going to keep playing the victim.

I wasn't going to keep begging for people who couldn't give a damn about me. I wasn't going to keep swallowing my pride for people who didn't even care enough to show up when it mattered.

One day, I stood in the shower, water pounding against me like a slap to the face, and I had an epiphany. The cold hit me like a punch to the gut, but it was like it was washing away everything—every single ounce of doubt, every moment I spent thinking I needed someone else to validate me.

The second I let that water hit me, it felt like everything was clearing out—every toxic person, every toxic thought, every ounce of emotional baggage.

And I came out of that shower a new fucking person.

I wasn't going to be that girl anymore. The one who kept begging for attention. The one who let people treat her like shit and still begged for more.

I wasn't going to be the one who let people pull me into their drama, their games, their bullshit. I was done with them.

I wasn't going to chase anyone ever again. I wasn't going to beg for love, beg for respect, beg for their damn approval. If you want to be in my life, you better show up. You better prove you're worthy. But if you're not? Get the fuck out. I'm not begging anyone for anything anymore.

So yeah, I made my comeback. But it wasn't a loud, dramatic entrance. It wasn't me knocking down doors or crying for attention. It was quiet, silent strength.

It was me not giving a damn anymore. It was me walking into every room like I owned it, not needing anyone's approval, not caring if they noticed. I didn't need them.

This time? I'm a force to be reckoned with. I'm not looking back. I'm not going to waste another minute on people who don't deserve a second of my time. I don't care if they regret it. I don't care if they miss me. I'm living for me now, and that's all that matters.

If they can't keep up, that's their fucking problem.

Because now? I'm my own hero.

LIVE YOUR LIFE, NOT THEIRS

There comes a point when you realize that no matter what you do, people will always have something to say. It doesn't matter if you play it safe or take risks—someone, somewhere, will have an opinion. So why bother shrinking yourself to fit their expectations?

I've met all kinds of people—some wise, some clueless, and some who exist purely to provide entertainment with their stupidity. You know the type.

There's the fearful ones—tiptoeing through life like they're defusing a bomb, terrified of what society might think. Spoiler alert: Society doesn't think. It just talks.

Then you have the phone-obsessed zombies—the ones glued to their screens like their soul will evaporate if they miss a single notification. Bro, it's just a meme. Chill.

And then, of course, there are the delusional billionaires—the ones drowning in financial chaos but flexing like they own a private jet. Your reality and your Instagram story are not the same thing, babe. Quit the act.

But my favorites? The rare, actually-sane people—the ones who prove that patience isn't weakness, that silence can slap harder than words, and that success is the loudest revenge.

Now, to the overthinkers who live in fear of opinions—get this through your head:

You have ONE life. Stop letting side characters write your story.

Those four jobless losers whispering about you? They don't care about you. You're just their latest free-time gossip until something shinier comes along. Let them talk. Their words won't pay your bills. Their opinions won't make you happy. So if you love something? If it fuels your soul? DO IT. LOUDLY.

And if someone has a problem? Hand them a tissue and tell them to go cry in a corner.

Now, let's talk about boomer aunties—the self-appointed moral police of society.

They'll judge you for wearing jeans—while standing there in a saree that's clinging on for dear life over their oversized, gravity-defying stomach rolls. The hypocrisy? Unmatched.

They never mind their own damn business. Instead, they sit in their tiny gossip circles, chewing on their dried-up opinions like it's their full-time job. And here's the hard truth:

They will talk NO MATTER WHAT.

Wear jeans? "Too modern."
Wear traditional clothes? "Trying too hard."
Breathe? Still not good enough.

So tell me, why waste a single second of your precious life trying to please people who will never be pleased? Let them choke on their own outdated expectations.

You? You keep rising. You keep winning. You keep living so unapologetically that their words burn before they even reach you.

And if anyone dares to question your choices? Just flash them a smile and say:

*"Oh, I didn't realize your approval was required for me to exist. My bad—let me continue not giving a f."**

Final words for my readers:
No matter where you come from, no matter how many people try to dim your fire, remember this—your life is yours.

People will always have opinions. Society will always have expectations. And obstacles? Oh, they'll show up like uninvited guests. But at the end of the day, you are the one who has to live with your choices.

So don't let fear, doubt, or pressure hold you back. Chase your dreams like a storm. Make mistakes. Learn. Grow. And most importantly—

Never settle for less than what you deserve.

One life. Live it on your terms.

THE UNSEEN LOVE

Growing up, I used to think love was all about grand gestures, sweet words, and friendships that promised forever.

But after experiencing betrayals from the people I trusted the most, I realized something—the purest, most unconditional love has always been right in front of me. My family.

My parents are stricter than you can imagine. Sometimes, I hated them for it.

The constant rules, the endless *"No, you can't do this,"* or *"That's not right for you."* It felt suffocating. I used to think, *Why can't they just let me live my life?* But as life unfolded, I started seeing things from their perspective.

Every single time they stopped me from doing something, they were not trying to control me—they were protecting me from something they knew I wouldn't see coming.

After all the betrayals, heartbreaks, and disappointments, I looked back and realized—if I had just listened to them, so many problems wouldn't have even existed in my life.

They had already warned me, but I was too stubborn to believe them. Because when we're young, we assume we know better.

We think our parents are too old-fashioned, too strict, too overprotective. But what we don't realize is that they have already seen the world in ways we haven't. They have experienced every emotion we are just beginning to understand—pain, love, loss, regret.

And my father—oh, how he used to warn me, *"Don't be too friendly with everyone. Keep a limit."* I would get so irritated. I could understand them warning me about love because, yeah, I fell for the wrong person.

But why even warn me about friendships? That felt unfair. But turns out, he was right. Even in friendships, I trusted the wrong people. I gave my all to people who didn't even deserve a fraction of it.

The ones I thought would stand by me forever were the same ones who stabbed me in the back when I needed them the most.

And now, I strongly believe that just blindly listening to my parents would have saved me from a lot of unnecessary heartbreak. They weren't against my happiness; they were just protecting me from the pain they already saw coming.

Then, there's my brother—10 years younger than me. And of course, as a child, I was insanely jealous of him. He got all the attention that was once mine. He was pampered, loved, and spoiled while I was expected to be the 'grown-up' one.

Sometimes, I would even fake being sick just so my mom would take care of me the way she cared for him. I craved that kind of love, the one that I didn't see every day but knew was there.

But I was wrong to ever think my mom and my brother didn't love me. When I went on my IV trip, both of them cried because I wasn't home for just three days.

Even my brother, who never shows emotions, missed me. That moment hit me hard—I saw their love in its purest form. They might not say it every day, they might not always express it the way I want, but their love is real.

"He" is my brother—the one I fight with, the one I love the most. There's a ten-year gap between us, yet I argue with him over the silliest things like we're equals. Every morning and evening, he stands at my bus stop with my mother, as if it's an unspoken duty.

I call him *Chettu*, even in the heat of an argument. No matter how angry I get, no matter how much I lose control of my words, his real name never comes out.

Maybe because *Chettu* isn't just a name—it's my way of holding on to him, a reminder that no fight, no anger, nothing can change the bond we share.

And he never gets distracted by his phone—ever. But the moment I start singing, he pauses, his gaze shifting from the screen to me, watching with a big smile on his face, as if my voice is the only thing that matters in that moment. He is my biggest admirer.

MOM VS. THE PHONE

And then, there's my mom. If I had to describe her in one sentence, I'd say—she has the sharpest tongue but the softest heart.

She scolds me every single day, and sometimes, I feel like she nags more than she talks. But who else has the right to? If she doesn't correct me, who will? If she doesn't guide me, who will? A mother's love is something we often misunderstand.

We get irritated when she yells at us for small things. We roll our eyes when she asks us too many questions. But the truth is, no one in this entire world will ever love you as selflessly as a mother does.

But… one thing that *still* annoys me? Privacy.

Privacy? What's That?

Privacy in my house? **A joke. A myth. A fantasy that doesn't exist in reality.**

You close your room door? **Suspicious.**

You take too long in the bathroom? **Highly suspicious.**

You smile at your phone? **National security threat.**

Do you sleep during the day? **Lazy.**

You wake up late? **Irresponsible.**
You stay silent? **Something's wrong.**
Do you talk too much? **Something's wrong.**
Basically, **you breathe? Something's wrong.**

There is no concept of *"me time"* in an Indian household. If you sit alone for too long, your mom will come and ask, *"What happened? Why are you so silent?"* If you talk too much, she'll say, *"Why are you shouting so much? Calm down!"*

Oh, and let's not forget that classic line. You've been sitting there, minding your own business, and then— *BAM*, the guilt trip starts.

"Why is it that when I ask you to do something, you act like the world's ending? You tell me, 'I have work to do,' or 'I'm busy,' but the second you pick up that phone, you're suddenly free to waste time! It's like you have all the time in the world to scroll through random stuff, but when it comes to helping out, you suddenly have 'no time.'"

Like, seriously? First off, you weren't even wasting time! You were just taking a break for a few minutes.

But of course, in her eyes, that's somehow more offensive than skipping an entire day of work. Suddenly, you're the villain in your own life story.

And the worst part? She doesn't even give you a chance to explain. Before you can even open your mouth, she's already going full throttle with the guilt.

"You think I'm just sitting around doing nothing all day?" she'll say, making you feel like you're the one who's been slacking off when you've been working your butt off the whole time.

It doesn't matter that you're literally drowning in assignments, tasks, and responsibilities. The second she sees you take a moment for yourself, that's when the "wasting time" accusations come flying at you, like you've committed some horrible crime.

She'll throw in a dramatic pause just to make sure you're sinking into the guilt like it's quicksand, and you're left wondering, *when did a 5-minute break become such a cardinal sin?*

All you wanted was a little time for yourself to recharge, and now, you've been branded as the lazy, unhelpful person who doesn't care about anything but their phone.

But of course, the guilt doesn't stop there. "You know, if you spent as much time helping me as you do wasting time on your phone, maybe we'd actually get things done around here."

It's like they know just how to press your buttons to make you feel like the worst person on earth for trying to have a single moment of peace.

Sometimes, I feel like I need a full-fledged *privacy policy agreement* to exist in my own house.

Because the moment I try to do something alone, my mom will magically appear out of nowhere, asking a hundred questions.

Ma, I know it may seem like I'm just sitting here, doing nothing. Maybe you think I'm wasting time, lost in my own world. But, Ma, I promise you—I'm not. I'm building something, shaping something that carries a piece of me in every word. I'm about to finish my book, Ma. A story born from my heart, my pain, my dreams.

I know you worry, I know you wonder if this is worth it. But one day, when you hold my book in your hands, when you see my name on it, you'll know—every second I spent here wasn't wasted. It was me, chasing something bigger than myself. Something I hope will make you proud.

But despite all the restrictions, all the scoldings, all the arguments—I wouldn't trade them for anything in this world.

Because at the end of the day, friends may come and go. Love may break and heal. But family? Family is forever.

Guiding with Grace

I like my parents, but some restrictions are just too much. I understand they want the best for me, that they worry, that they want to protect me from the world. But sometimes, their love feels more like a cage than a shelter.

When restrictions cross a limit, they don't just shape a child's behavior; they suffocate their spirit. It starts with small things—where you go, who you talk to, what you wear.

Then, it grows into something bigger—having no voice in your own life, feeling like your dreams don't matter, or constantly living in fear of disappointing them.

I have seen kids who hide things from their parents, not because they want to do something wrong, but because they know they won't be understood.

I have seen young people who lose themselves, who become strangers in their own homes, simply because they were never allowed to be who they really are.

Advice to Young Parents

Love should be about trust, not control. A child who feels heard will never turn away. But one who grows up in chains will one day break free, even if it means walking far from the home they once loved.

Understand that your children are individuals, not just extensions of you. Guide them, but don't dictate every step. Listen to their dreams, even if they seem unrealistic. Let them make mistakes, learn, and grow.

Being a parent isn't about owning your child's life; it's about preparing them to live it on their own. Give them the space to breathe, to explore, to be themselves—because a happy child will always come back home, but a caged one will only look for an escape.

Life's Too Short to Be Complicated

I have a lot of changes in my life right now, and also, I've come to realize one simple truth—**we make life way harder than it needs to be.**

If there is a fight, just say *sorry*. If you want to talk to someone, just *call*. If you miss someone, just *convey it*. If you love someone, just *confess it*. Overthinking ruins everything, and trust me, no one has time for unnecessary complications.

I used to be the kind of person who would bottle up my emotions, waiting for the *perfect* moment. But life doesn't wait for anyone.

The people you love won't be around forever, and sometimes, holding back only leads to regret.

Let me tell you a story. There was a girl who always hesitated. If she had a fight with someone, she'd wait for the other person to apologize first. If she missed a friend, she'd convince herself *"Maybe they don't miss me back."*

If she wanted to confess her feelings, she'd think *"What if they reject me?"*

She kept waiting for the *right time*, but time never waited for her.

Eventually, people moved on, opportunities slipped away, and she was left with nothing but *what-ifs*.

One day, she decided to change. She picked up her phone and texted that one friend she hadn't spoken to in months. She apologized first, even when her ego screamed not to.

She finally told someone she loved them, without worrying about the outcome. And you know what? Nothing bad happened. In fact, life felt *lighter*. She stopped carrying unnecessary burdens and just started *living*.

At the end of the day, **life is short, but regrets last forever**. So stop making things complicated. If you want something, *go for it*. If you love someone, *show them*. If you're sorry, *say it*.

Because the worst thing isn't rejection or failure—**it's never trying at all.**

This world never stops judging—no matter what you do. Smile at someone? They might take it the wrong way. Offer a handshake? Somehow, that could be a mistake too. And yet, the same people who judge will claim they're only doing it for your safety.

So, live on your terms. Be good, but don't let anyone walk over you. In the end, it's your life, your choices, and your happiness that matter.

THE MARK YOU LEAVE

People enter our lives for different reasons, sometimes as a blessing, sometimes as a lesson, and sometimes as both. Some come to show us love, to remind us of kindness, to bring light into our darkest moments. Others arrive to teach us strength, to challenge us, or to break us just enough that we grow into someone we never imagined we could be.

Some people are meant to stay forever, becoming a part of our journey, shaping our happiness, and walking beside us no matter what. Others are temporary—meant to cross our path, leave their mark, and then move on. And that's okay.

Every person who enters our life plays a role. Some teach us patience, some teach us pain, and some teach us what we deserve. The trick is knowing when to hold on and when to let go, when to learn from them and when to walk away. Because no one enters our life without a purpose, but not everyone is meant to stay.

Decide who you want to be in someone's life—a blessing or a lesson, a light or a shadow. Do you want to be the one who brings warmth, who lifts them up, who stands by them even when the world turns cold? Or do you want to be the one they remember with pain, the one who taught them what betrayal feels like?

You have the power to be someone's safe place, their reason to smile, the person who shows them what love, kindness, and loyalty truly mean. But you also have the choice to be the one who makes them guard their heart, the one who turns their softness into stone.

At the end of the day, you decide. Will you be the person they cherish forever or the one they had to heal from? Because no matter what, you will leave a mark—make sure it's one worth remembering.

Know Your Worth

Before anything else, before love, before friendships, before even your dreams—you must know your worth. Because the moment you forget it, the world will try to convince you that you are less.

People will make you feel like you have to prove yourself, like you have to earn their love, their respect, their time. But the truth? You never have to beg to be valued.

The right people will see your worth without you having to remind them. The wrong ones will only stay if you keep lowering yourself to fit their expectations.

There will be moments when you feel like staying silent is easier, when shrinking yourself feels safer. But don't. Never let the fear of losing someone make you lose yourself. Your kindness is not a weakness. Your love is not a debt. And your presence is not a privilege someone else gets to control.

Nothing in this world is more important than you. Not the opinions of those who don't appreciate you. Not the love of someone who takes you for granted. Not the validation of people who only see your value when it benefits them.

Stand tall. Speak loud. And if someone cannot respect you, don't waste a second proving your worth—just walk away. Because once you know your value, you will never accept anything less than what you deserve.

It's okay to make life easier, to choose peace over struggle—
but never at the cost of yourself. Prioritize yourself first,
always.

Forgive, But Never Forget

Forgiveness is powerful. It frees you from the weight of anger, from the endless cycle of pain that keeps replaying in your mind. It's a gift—not for them, but for you. But there's a difference between forgiving and lowering yourself to be walked on.

People will hurt you. Some will apologize, some won't. Some will mean it, some will never change. You might find it in your heart to let go of the pain, but that doesn't mean you have to let them stay.

Respect yourself enough to know when to walk away. When someone shatters your trust, when they treat you as if you are replaceable, when they expect you to forgive but refuse to change—that is where you draw the line.

Forgiveness is not an invitation to be mistreated again. It is not a weakness, nor is it an obligation. It is your way of saying, *"I release this burden, but I will never let it happen again."* You can forgive and still demand better. You can move on and still refuse to let history repeat itself.

Never mistake self-respect for pride. There is nothing wrong with expecting to be treated right. There is nothing wrong with choosing peace over toxic people. Forgive, but never at the cost of your worth. Because the moment you give that up, you are no longer forgiving—you are losing yourself.

Forgiveness is a gift you give yourself. It's not about excusing what someone did, nor is it about pretending the pain never existed.

It's about releasing the weight of anger so it no longer controls you. Because carrying resentment is like holding fire in your hands—it only burns you.

But forgiving does not mean forgetting. It doesn't mean allowing the same hurt to happen again. It doesn't mean reopening doors that were meant to stay closed. Pain teaches lessons, and those lessons are not meant to be erased.

Remember who hurt you. Remember what it taught you. Remember how it changed you. Because forgetting means risking history repeating itself.

So forgive, but never forget. Move forward, but never step back into the same fire. Some wounds heal, but the scars remain to remind you of what you survived. Let them make you wiser, not weaker.

THE SHADOW THAT FOLLOWS

There was a time when envy clung to me like a shadow I couldn't shake. Every time I scrolled through my phone, I saw people who seemed happier, luckier.

Friends traveling the world while I was stuck in the same place. Strangers achieving things I only dared to dream about. Their victories felt like my failures. Their happiness made me question my own.

It made me question my own journey, made me forget that my life wasn't meant to be a copy of someone else's.

One day, I caught myself staring at a picture of someone I barely knew, feeling that same familiar sting of comparison. But this time, instead of letting it consume me, I stopped. I asked myself, *Why am I letting someone else's success make me feel like less?* Their life had nothing to do with mine. Their wins didn't mean my loss. I was fighting a battle that wasn't even real.

That was the moment I decided to change.

I stood in front of my mirror and really looked at myself. *Shalu, you have everything,* I told myself. *You are beautiful. You are talented. You have things others only wish they had.* I thought about my long, black hair—something many girls wished for.

My accent, which stood out while others struggled with an ordinary one.My talents—I could sing, dance, cook, and understand things easily, and if I wished to learn something new, I knew I could master it.

 I had freedom, not completely, but enough to know that after I finished my degree, I would do everything I had ever dreamed of.

And in that moment, something shifted.

Jealousy didn't have power over me anymore. Because when I looked at myself—not through the lens of what I lacked, but through the truth of everything I already had—I felt whole. I felt enough.

Jealousy is a thief. It steals your joy, your confidence, your peace. But only if you let it. The truth is, the more I started clapping for others, the lighter I felt. The more I focused on my own growth, the less I cared about what anyone else was doing.

And now? Now, when I see someone winning, I smile. Because I know their success doesn't take away from mine. And because I finally understand—what's meant for me will always find its way to me, no matter how long it takes.

And if there ever comes a moment when envy tries to creep in again, I'll stand in front of my mirror and remind myself: *I already have everything I need to shine.*

THE UNSEEN WEALTH

There is something everyone possesses—rich or poor, young or old. It is given freely, yet most people waste it without realizing its value. This unseen wealth is *time*. Unlike money, it cannot be saved.

Unlike lost opportunities, it never returns. And those who fail to use it wisely often wonder why success never knocks on their door.

Procrastination is the silent thief that steals dreams. It starts with small excuses—*just five more minutes, I'll do it tomorrow, now isn't the right time*—until days turn into months and months into years.

Goals remain unachieved, ideas remain mere thoughts, and life moves forward, leaving the unprepared behind.

But those who rise above procrastination understand one truth: time waits for no one. They do not wait for motivation to strike or for the perfect moment to begin.

They take the first step, however small it may be. The hardest part is starting, but once the momentum builds, progress becomes unstoppable.

The mind, when left unchecked, seeks comfort. It tricks one into believing that there is always more time. But the secret to overcoming this trap is discipline.

A task started is already half won. The body resists, but action silences doubt. Planning helps, but execution is what turns dreams into reality.

Each day presents a choice—to waste time or to use it wisely. The ones who understand this, who push forward despite distractions, are the ones who carve their names into history.

Because in the end, success is not built in a day, but in the moments that were not wasted.

MOTIVATION IS A SCAM

When we're broke, lost, or trying to pick ourselves up, we turn to motivational videos. We sit there, watching success stories, hearing words that make us feel like *yes, I can do this too*. For a moment, we feel unstoppable.

Let's be real—motivation is the biggest scam of the century. You sit there, wasting hours watching "life-changing" videos, feeling pumped for five minutes, and then what? **Back to scrolling, back to excuses, back to nothing.**

The truth? **If you need motivation to start, you'll never make it.**

You don't need another fancy speech. You don't need a guru telling you to "believe in yourself." What you need is to stop bullshitting yourself and **start moving.**

Motivation is a lie. It fades. It's weak. **Discipline is the real game-changer.** The ones who win? They don't wait to "feel ready." They don't need a hype-up session. They just **do it.** Whether they feel like it or not.

So, stop sitting there, waiting for some magical push. No one is coming to save you. No video, no quote, no book will do the work for you. **Only you can.**

Decide. Move. Execute. Repeat.

Because in the end, motivation is just noise. **Action is the only thing that counts.**

THE HEALING POWER OF NATURE

There comes a point where you decide you've had enough—enough of feeling stuck, enough of drowning in self-doubt, enough of carrying the weight of things that no longer serve you.

You know it's time for a comeback, but where do you even begin? The answer isn't in a book, a motivational speech, or even within yourself.

Sometimes, the answer is all around you—in the wind, the rain, the stars, the mountains.

Nature has a way of whispering truths we often ignore. **The sky never holds onto a storm forever. The wind never clings to a single direction. The ocean never stops moving.**

Everything flows, everything changes, and maybe that's the sign you need—it's time to move forward.

Think about the **clouds.** They drift effortlessly, shaping and reshaping, never clinging to a single form. They don't fight the wind, they **go with it.**

And yet, no matter how many times they disappear, they always return.

Why do we, as humans, hold onto things so tightly when even the sky itself keeps changing?

And then there's the **rain.** It doesn't just cleanse the earth, it cleanses the soul. There's a reason people stand in the rain when they feel lost—it's nature's way of **washing away the past.**

It doesn't ask you to be strong, it doesn't ask you to hide. It simply lets you feel. It lets you start over.

The **ocean?** It never fights back, it never resists. It rises, it falls, it flows with life's rhythm. And maybe that's what we should do too.

Instead of overthinking every little thing, instead of stressing over what's out of our control, maybe we should learn to just **ride the waves.**

And when you feel small, when your struggles seem too big, look up at the **stars.** They've been burning bright for millions of years, watching civilizations rise and fall, watching people come and go.

And here you are, worrying about things that won't even matter a year from now. **Your problems aren't as permanent as they feel.**

Nature teaches the most important lesson of all: **nothing is permanent, not even your struggles.** The trees don't force their leaves to grow. The flowers don't rush to bloom.

The rivers don't struggle to find their way to the ocean. Yet, everything happens in its own time. Maybe that's the secret—to **trust the process, to breathe, to exist, to let go, and to let life happen.**

Or, maybe... **just put your phone down and enjoy nature for once. Most of your problems could end right there.**

Fear Fades When You Face It

Listen, I get it. That fear of standing in front of people, the awkwardness when all eyes are on you—it's real. It makes your heart race, your hands shake, and your mind go blank.

You start thinking, *What if I mess up? What if people laugh?* But let me tell you something—most people aren't even paying as much attention as you think.

You see, confidence isn't about being fearless. It's about doing it anyway, despite the fear. The more you put yourself out there, the less scary it becomes.

The first time will feel like a disaster. The second time? A little better. By the tenth time, you'll wonder why you were ever scared at all.

And awkward moments? They happen to everyone. The difference is, confident people don't let it define them. You stutter? Keep going. You say something weird? Laugh it off. Nobody remembers small mistakes as much as you do. In fact, when you own the moment, people respect you even more.

One more thing—stop thinking about *yourself* so much. Focus on what you're saying, not on how you look or sound. The moment you shift your focus from *How do I seem?* to *What do I want to say?*, everything changes.

So don't wait to feel 'ready.' Just start. Speak up. Show up. Keep doing it until the fear shrinks into something so small, it no longer controls you. Because trust me—one day, you'll look back and realize the only thing stopping you was *you*.

Confidence Looks Like Arrogance to the Insecure

If I care, I care **like hell.** I go all in—no half-assed loyalty, no fake smiles, no pretending. But if I don't? Then I don't give a **single f*ck.** Simple. You either get **everything** or **nothing.** There's no middle ground with me.

And yet, people love to call me "arrogant." Why? Because I don't beg for validation? Because I don't waste time on irrelevant people? Because I don't dumb myself down to make them feel comfortable?

Nah, let's call it what it is—I'm just **not easy to manipulate.**

They say I have an attitude? **Damn right, I do.** It's called standards. It's called not tolerating half-hearted friendships, one-sided efforts, and people who switch up when it's convenient.

My energy isn't a free trial—it's **exclusive access.** You earn it, or you get locked out. Period.

I don't chase. I don't explain myself to people who are committed to misunderstanding me. If I walk away, I don't come back. **No second chances. No rewrites. No closure.** You lost me? That's your problem, not mine.

They say I'm "too much"? Nah. They're just **too weak.**

Too used to fake people, too comfortable with mediocrity, too intimidated by someone who actually knows their worth. The truth is, I was never **too much**—they were just **never enough.**

So yeah, they thought I was arrogant. Until they realized I was the **best thing they never deserved.** And by then? I was already gone.

Girls, my dear darlings, who set these damn rules? Who decided what a "girl" should walk like, talk like, act like? Who made the rulebook that says we have to be soft-spoken, polite, delicate little things? **Newsflash: That book? We're setting it on fire.**

Walk how you want. Talk how you want. Be loud, be quiet, be bold, be wild, be fierce, be messy—**be whatever the hell you want.** Wear heels, wear sneakers, wear combat boots— hell, walk barefoot if that's what makes you feel free.

They told us to be graceful, to be "lady-like." But why? To make others comfortable? To fit into some outdated mold? **Nah, not happening.**

You are not here to be **pleasing.** You are not here to be **approved.** You are not here to fit inside their pretty little box.

And if you want to feel secure in this society, **carry what you need, learn what you must.** A pepper spray, a pocket knife, brass knuckles—hell, even your house key between your fingers if you have to.

Better yet, learn self-defense. Learn how to throw a punch, how to fight back, how to make sure no one ever sees you as an easy target.

Because strength isn't just in your attitude—it's in your actions. It's in knowing that no matter what, you can **stand your ground.**

Girls, **do whatever you like.** Run the world, break the rules, speak your mind, chase your dreams, take up space, own your power. **Be unstoppable.** Be **you.**

Because this world doesn't need another "perfect" girl. It needs **real ones.**

Finding Joy in the Little Things

Sometimes, we get so caught up in our frustrations and the problems around us that we forget to notice the little joys in life. We wait for something big, something grand, to make us happy—but happiness doesn't always come wrapped in fireworks.

Find happiness in small things—just like I do. Sounds crazy, right? But listen, I don't wait for life to hand me some perfect moment to feel alive.

I don't sit around hoping happiness will knock on my door one day.

Instead, I find it in the warmth of the morning sun, in the way the breeze plays with my hair, in the sound of my favorite song on a rainy evening, or even in the laughter shared over silly conversations.

Life is full of struggles, and yes, some days feel impossible. But if we only focus on the pain, we'll miss the beauty that still exists around us. So take a deep breath, slow down, and notice the little things.

A kind word, a good book, a moment of peace—happiness is everywhere, you just have to see it.

I find it in the simplest things. Like when I make the perfect cup of coffee, and that first sip hits just right. Or when the sky, out of nowhere, turns gloomy on a scorching summer day, wrapping the world in a quiet, mysterious mood.

It's in these little moments where real happiness hides—while most people waste their lives chasing something bigger, something *more.*

We've been tricked into thinking happiness is some grand prize at the finish line—waiting for us after we land the perfect job, the perfect partner, the perfect life. But the truth? Happiness isn't some distant destination.

It's not locked behind "one day" or "after I achieve this." It's right here, right now, slipping through your fingers while you're too busy searching for something **better.**

I used to believe I needed something more to feel complete.

Maybe, if I checked off all the right boxes, I'd finally feel content. But then, there were moments that made me realize happiness isn't found in *more,* it's found in the things we take for granted.

Like the day I got my own phone—finally, a little piece of freedom in my hands. It wasn't just about having a device; it was the feeling of independence, the excitement of something that was *mine.*

And then, there's *this* moment—right now—as I write the final words of this book, knowing I've checked off one of the biggest dreams on my bucket list.

I did it.

I turned my thoughts into words, my pain into power, my experiences into something that will live beyond me. And that? That's happiness.

Most people are blind to it. They think they'll be happy *once they have more.* More money, more success, more love—more of whatever they think will fill the void inside them.

But the truth? **More will never be enough if you can't appreciate what's already in front of you.**

Happiness is in the things you overlook every damn day. It's in the way the night breeze feels on your skin.

It's in the music that hits differently at 2 a.m. It's in the quiet moments, the unexpected laughter, the way the world slows down when you actually stop and look around.

You're not unhappy because life is bad. You're unhappy because you refuse to see the beauty in the simple things.

You've trained yourself to believe that happiness is a distant dream instead of a choice you can make every single second.

So, stop waiting. Stop chasing. Stop believing the lie that happiness is somewhere *out there.* It's **here.** It's in the unnoticed, the ordinary, the quiet magic of life itself.

And if you keep waiting for some grand event to bring you joy, you'll miss the millions of little moments that would have already made you feel alive.

Unshakable Mindset

The subconscious mind is the most powerful tool we have, yet most of us never realize its true potential. It controls our habits, our reactions, our beliefs—shaping our lives in ways we don't even notice.

Every thought we repeat, every emotion we feed, every belief we hold onto sinks deep into our subconscious, quietly directing our actions.

Have you ever noticed how certain things feel effortless? The way you tie your shoes without thinking, how you navigate familiar streets without needing directions, or how your body wakes up at the same time every morning? That's your subconscious at work.

But it's not just about habits—it's about everything. If you constantly tell yourself you're not good enough, your subconscious will make sure you act like it.

If you believe you're meant for greatness, your subconscious will find ways to push you toward it.

The problem is, most of us program our subconscious with negativity. We doubt ourselves, we replay past failures, we let fear take over.

And then we wonder why things never change. The truth? Your mind believes whatever you feed it.

You tell yourself you're unlucky, and you'll start noticing only the bad. You tell yourself you can't do something, and suddenly, every challenge feels impossible.

But the moment you start feeding your subconscious with confidence, with belief, with the idea that you deserve everything you want—things shift.

And one rule? Never lower yourself in front of anyone. Stop saying bad things about yourself, even as a joke. The way you speak about yourself matters more than you think. If you keep calling yourself weak, unlucky, or unworthy, your subconscious will believe it and shape your reality around it.

Speak highly of yourself, even if you're still growing. If someone compliments you, don't brush it off—take it. Own it. You deserve to be recognized, so stop feeling shy about it.

I've seen this power in my own life. The moment I got my own phone, something changed. It wasn't just about having a device—it was about independence, freedom, the feeling of finally crossing off something from my bucket list.

And now, finishing this book? That's another dream turned into reality. These weren't just random events; they were things I had imagined, things I had told myself I would achieve, and my subconscious found a way to make them happen.

Your mind is either your greatest enemy or your biggest ally. Train it wisely. Fill it with belief. Let it work for you, not against you.

Because once your subconscious mind aligns with your desires, nothing in this world can stop you.

HARD SHELL, SOFTCORE

People always assume I'm tough. And honestly? I don't blame them. I walk like I own the ground beneath my feet, talk like I've got nothing to lose, and stare people down just enough to make them rethink their choices. Confidence? Nah, it's just how I am. Or at least, that's what I let them believe.

Most people don't bother looking past the surface. They see the sharp words, the smirks, the unbothered attitude, and they think, *Damn, this one's heartless.* I don't correct them. It's easier that way. Keeps unnecessary drama out of my life. But the funny part? The same people who call me "scary" are the ones who come running when they need someone to stand up for them.

Once, someone actually admitted it to my face. "You know, you're kind of terrifying," they said with a nervous laugh. "But, like, in a good way?" I just raised an eyebrow. A *good* way? What does that even mean? Turns out, they meant reliable. Unshakable. The kind of person who doesn't fold under pressure.

What they don't see is the other side—the side that overthinks at 2 AM, the side that holds onto old memories, the side that still believes in love despite everything. But that's the thing. Just because I've got a soft spot doesn't mean I'm weak. It means I know exactly when to let my guard down and when to keep it up. It means I pick my battles, and when I fight, I don't lose.

So yeah, keep thinking I'm untouchable. Keep believing I don't feel a thing. Because when I do? That's when you'll really understand what I'm made of.

THE POWER YOU HOLD

People talk. Oh, they love to talk—especially when they think I'm not listening. They whisper behind my back, throwing little jabs, making up stories, trying so hard to define me. And why? Because I'm not like them. Because I don't fit into their little idea of how a person should be.

Yeah, I'm different. I don't fake smiles just to be liked. I don't follow the crowd just to feel included. I don't tone myself down to make others comfortable. And that? That scares them. So, they do what weak people always do—talk in the shadows, hoping their words might shake me.

But here's the funny part: not one of them has the courage to say it to my face. Not one. They'll look me in the eye, nod, smile, pretend like they've got nothing to say—because deep down, they know. They know I see through them. They know I don't need their approval. And they know that if they ever dared to bring their little stories to me, I'd shut them down so fast they wouldn't know what hit them.

That's the power you hold when you stop seeking validation. When you stop explaining yourself. When you realize that the noise behind you doesn't matter. You become untouchable. You become someone they can't figure out, can't break, can't control.

So, let them talk. Let them whisper. At the end of the day, their words don't define me. **I do.**

Fear the Beast Within

People are scared of ghosts. Some freak out over heights. And a few cry over cockroaches. But me? I only fear one thing—**myself.**

No joke. Have you ever seen me when I decide to **change?** When will I go all in? It's **game over** for everyone.

Once, someone straight-up told me, **"You actually scare me."**

I just smirked. *Damn right.*

Because when I flip that switch, I don't just step up—I **take over.** No second thoughts, no hesitations. Just pure, **unapologetic** energy. And people? Oh, they feel it. They see it. And they start sweating.

Because they know—once I decide to move? **No one's stopping me.**

So if you're ever gonna be afraid of something, **make sure it's you.** Because the moment you **stop fearing failure, rejection, or what people think,** you don't just become dangerous.

You become **unstoppable.**

NOT THE END, BUT MY BEGINNING

Each and every word here? It comes from my own experience. These aren't just empty lines meant to sound inspiring—they are the truth I lived, the lessons I learned, the things that pulled me from the depths and pushed me toward success.

I have known the power of time—the way it slips away from those who waste it and rewards those who use it wisely.

I have learned that patience is not just a virtue, but a weapon, a silent force that turns struggles into victories.

Confidence? It wasn't something I was born with. It was something I built, brick by brick, refusing to let self-doubt and the judgments of others decide my worth.

I have walked through betrayal, through heartbreak, through moments where giving up seemed easier than going on. But I refused. I did not let the past bury me.

I did not let pain define me. Every lie told to me, every time I was underestimated, every time someone thought I would stay broken—it all became fuel. It sharpened me into someone unshakable.

I stopped waiting for miracles and started creating them. I stopped shrinking for others, stopped dimming my fire because someone else couldn't handle its heat. I claimed every victory, big or small. I embraced my worth without apology.

The world does not hand power to those who wait, to those who whisper, to those who let themselves be broken beyond repair. It belongs to those who rise, who refuse to beg, who own their story instead of being destroyed by it.

And here I am, standing at the end of these pages but at the beginning of something even greater.

I hold my own book in my hands—something I once only dreamed of finishing. And this? This is just the start.

To those who betrayed me, to those who doubted me, to those who thought I would stay the same forever—watch closely. Because I haven't even begun to shine.

This isn't the end of my story. This is my beginning.

To the girl I used to be—the one who loved too deeply, trusted too blindly, and broke too hard. You didn't deserve the pain, but you survived it. And that survival? That's your power.

To the ones who lied, betrayed, and walked away—you thought you destroyed me. But all you did was set me free. I don't hate you. I thank you. Because without you, I would've never found the fire that now burns inside me.

To the people who underestimated me, laughed at my dreams, and thought I'd never make it—you fueled a storm that will never settle. Watch me.

To the girl I hurt the most—the one I abandoned, doubted, and silenced just to keep others happy. The one I should've protected instead of breaking her down. I'm sorry. I see you now, and I promise, I will never let you down again.

And to you—the one reading this, the one who has been shattered, the one who wonders if they'll ever be whole again. You will. But not by waiting for someone to save you.

You will rise the moment you decide that no one—not the past, not the pain, not the people who left—gets to write your ending.

This is not where the story stops.
This is where you take the pen.

This is the rebirth.

A NOTE TO MY READER

To the one holding this book—you are stronger than you think. Life may have tested you, betrayed you, and left you questioning your worth. I know that pain. I've walked through it, too. But let me remind you: you are not what happened to you. You are what you choose to become.

This book is more than words on paper. It's proof that no matter how broken you feel, you can rise. No matter who left, you are still whole. No matter how many times life knocks you down, you have the power to stand back up— taller, wiser, and unstoppable.

So walk like you own the ground beneath your feet. Carry yourself with the confidence of someone who knows they are enough. Forgive, but never forget. Adapt, but never lose yourself. And when the world doubts you—don't argue, don't explain. Just succeed.

Your story isn't over. It's only just beginning.
 Make it powerful. Make it legendary.

With strength and love,
Shalu

"Life ah mathanumnu mudivu panniyachu.
Inimel enna aanalum pathukalamnu
poitey irukanum.

Unna meeri edhuvum nadakadhu.
Idhu namma kaalam. Erangi adi!"